THE MINI ROUGH GUIDE TO
MADEIRA

T0015967

ROUGH
GUIDES

YOUR TAILOR-MADE TRIP STARTS HERE

Tailor-made trips and unique adventures crafted by local experts

Rough Guides has been inspiring travellers for more than 35 years. Leave it to our local experts to create your perfect itinerary and book it at local rates.

Don't follow the crowd – find your own path.

HOW ROUGHGUIDES.COM/TRIPS WORKS

STEP 1 Pick your dream destination, tell us what you want and submit an enquiry.

STEP 2 Fill in a short form to tell your local expert about your dream trip and preferences.

STEP 3 Our local expert will craft your tailor-made itinerary. You'll be able to tweak and refine it until you're completely satisfied.

STEP 4 Book online with ease, pack your bags and enjoy the trip! Our local expert will be on hand 24/7 while you're on the road.

PLAN AND BOOK YOUR TRIP AT
ROUGHGUIDES.COM/TRIPS

HOW TO DOWNLOAD YOUR FREE EBOOK

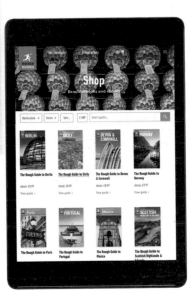

1. Visit **www.roughguides. com/free-ebook** or scan the **QR code** below

2. Enter the code **madeira945**

3. Follow the simple step-by-step instructions

For troubleshooting contact: mail@roughguides.com

10 THINGS NOT TO MISS

1. **MADEIRA'S HILLS AND MOUNTAINS**
Venture out on spectacular scenic walks. See page 58.

2. **THE ADEGAS DE SÃO FRANCISCO**
Visit the oldest working wine lodge in Madeira. See page 29.

3. **MONTE**
The fashionable hilltop town above Funchal is best known for its exhilarating toboggan rides. See page 41.

4. **JARDIM BOTÂNICO**
Marvel at Madeira's extravagant flowers. See page 39.

5. **PICO DO ARIEIRO**
Drive above the clouds to the top of Madeira's second-highest peak. See page 56.

6. **FUNCHAL'S MUSEU DE ARTE SACRA**
Outstanding Flemish paintings enjoy pride of place in this museum. See page 32.

7. **PORTO SANTO**
Relax on gorgeous golden sands on this nearby island. See page 66.

8. **MADEIRA'S LIDO COMPLEXES**
Enjoy a dip. See page 89.

9. **PALHEIRO COTTAGES**
These traditional thatched cottages are still in use in the Santana region. See page 60.

10. **SÃO VICENTE**
One of Madeira's most attractive villages, with volcanic caves nearby. See page 53.

A PERFECT TOUR

Day 1

Funchal finery. Split your first day in the capital Funchal between the magnificent Quinta das Cruzes and the Adegas de Sao Francisco, the historic wine lodge. In the former, you can check out the antiques and faded splendour of one of Funchal's grandest mansions, and in the latter, you can taste Madeira's extraordinary fortified wines.

Day 2

Cable car and market. Still in Funchal, take in the amazing views via one of Madeira's cable car routes, either from the base station in Old Town or from the Jardim Botânico (explore the gardens first if you choose the latter). Both go to Monte and offer return journeys. Next, browse your way around the Mercado dos Lavradores, a busy, colourful spectacle, with leather goods, wickerwork, and handicrafts on sale alongside fruit, vegetables and fish.

Day 3

Wicker toboggans. It's a short hop by road to the hilltop town of Monte, where you can explore the many local gardens, such as Jardim do Palácio do Monte, and indulge in a traditional downhill wicker toboggan ride, aided by drivers dressed in straw boaters.

Day 4

Hill gardens. Spend the day exploring the Palheiro Gardens, the most magnificent of Madeira's many splendid gardens. The hill-draped estate is a short bus ride from Funchal, and famous for its exotic plants, wild ravine, and gorgeous winter camellias.

OF **MADEIRA**

Day 5

Pico do Arieiro. You can take a bus tour to the summit of Madeira's third highest mountain, Pico do Arieiro in the central highlands of the island. It's something of a moonscape, whose plunging barren volcanic landscapes glow russet red in the sunlight.

Day 6

Nuns' refuge. Next, head to the equally spectacular Curral das Freiras, which you can reach via bus, car or organised tour, a 10km (6-mile) trip from Monte into another world. The village's name means 'Refuge of the Nuns', and it's encircled by a ring of mountains and was for a long time barely accessible to the outside world. It's an extraordinary sight, with the steep slopes around it dotted with terraces.

Day 7

São Vicente. The enchanting prettiness of São Vicente is worth the cross-island trip from Funchal. Not only will you see one of Madeira's most picturesque villages, but if you're feeling adventurous you can drive the heart-stopping, dazzling old coastal road from here to Porto Moniz.

Day 8

Porto Santo. On the last day of your trip, fly or boat over to the island of Porto Santo, with its 9km (5.6 miles) of golden beach. This tiny, mountainous, white-sand-fringed island is the ideal place to relax and spend the last day or so of your holiday.

CONTENTS

HIGHLIGHTS

A NOTE TO READERS

OVERVIEW

A mere speck in the middle of the Atlantic Ocean, Madeira is thickly draped with vegetation, a colourful riot of flowers and fruit trees. Rugged mountains peek through the clouds, and microclimates hover over isolated villages. Spectacular cliffs crash down to the surf below.

Although the islands were known to Roman and Carthaginian sailors 2,000 years ago, Madeira was only settled a few decades before Columbus made his way to America. It became part of the Portuguese empire after the great expedition teams of the fifteenth century claimed it for King João I. But Madeira is nearer to Africa than to Lisbon. It lies 600km (372 miles) off the coast of Morocco and nearly 1,000km (620 miles) southwest of the Portuguese capital.

Madeira is an archipelago, formed from volcanic eruptions many millions of years ago. The land is like an iceberg; massive mountains poke through the clouds, forming the mere tip of a submerged mass. Apart from Madeira itself, only one other island in the group is inhabited – the arid, much flatter holiday hideaway of Porto Santo. Christopher Columbus visited Porto Santo in the second half of the fifteenth century, and married the local governor's granddaughter.

NATURAL WONDERS

Few places on earth can rival Madeira's wealth of natural gifts, especially in so small an area. The island is blanketed with flowers: birds of paradise display their bright orange, beak-like flowers in open fields. Fragrant hydrangeas line walking paths skirting the edges of mountain terraces. Private and public gardens burst with orchids, bougainvillea and jacaranda trees, while orchards and plantations heave with apples, pears, cherries, passion fruit, bananas and avocados.

In the mountains, water streams down from unseen springs: a one-hour walk might take you past half a dozen waterfalls. The cold waters around the island, once prime whaling territory, are now a marine sanctuary for whales, dolphins and seals. And all of this in year-round sub-tropical weather, with a southerly breeze and temperatures that average 22°C (72°F) in the summer and 17°C (63°F) during the winter.

Waterfalls dot the interior

SIZE AND POPULATION

Madeira seems much larger than its diminutive size, just 57km (35 miles) long and 22km (13 miles) wide. The terrain is so mountainous, and its roads so tortuous, that distances are magnified in terms of both time and effort. This can breed insularity: before fast roads were constructed, some villagers never travelled to the capital, Funchal (pronounced 'foon-shawl'), let alone to mainland Portugal. Young and upwardly mobile islanders go off to seek their fortune – the most successful return from overseas and build sumptuous villas.

But Madeira is not a simple Gauguin-like tropical paradise. With a history of emigration and return, of welcoming visiting merchants and, during a brief period of occupation, a garrison of British troops, islanders are a cosmopolitan mix. The populace is a stew of dark North African complexions and blonde, blue-eyed northern Europeans.

THE CAPITAL CITY

Funchal, the island's capital, major harbour and only city of any note, merely hints at Madeira's riches. The capital's white houses with tile roofs are clustered on picturesque hills sloping down to a steep bay, which makes for a pretty picture. The city is undeniably pleasant, but there are parts of town where the noise and traffic

DESERTAS AND SELVAGENS

As well as the two inhabited islands of Madeira and Porto Santo, the North Atlantic archipelago comprises another five uninhabited islands and numerous minor rocks and reefs. The islands fall into two groups: the Ilhas Desertas (Desert Islands) and the Ilhas Selvagens (Wild or Savage Islands).

The former consists of three islands, the nearest situated 12km (19 miles) southeast of Madeira. These desert islands are far from the Robinson Crusoe idyll: they are barren and inhospitable to the point where, aside from the occasional goat and rabbit, the most notable land creature is a large, poisonous black spider.

But the sea life around the islands is a different story. Dolphins and turtles are occasionally spotted, and there is a colony of very rare monk seals. Bird-watchers will relish the opportunity to see shearwaters and petrels. Marine biologists and nature conservationists are the only regular human visitors, for even though excursion boats frequently make trips to these isles in summer, landing is restricted to authorised persons only.

Meanwhile, the two Selvagens Islands, usually known as Grande (Large) and Pequena (Small), are Madeiran only in name. They lie 285km (177 miles) to the south and are actually closer to the Canary Islands than to Madeira. Like the Desertas, they are uninhabited and devoted entirely to nature conservation.

don't seem so far removed from the places most people come here to avoid.

Almost half of Madeira's 270,000-strong population live in Funchal, where most of the island's tourism activity is centred. Here, visitors have a choice between the gleaming high-rise hotels of the *zona turista*, or the old-world hotels and distinguished *quintas* (rural estates) of Madeira's more peaceful past.

Funchal is a major harbour

THE RURAL INTERIOR

Funchal is less the sum of Madeira, though, than a gateway to the rest of the island, whose real charms begin in the hillsides just a few minutes outside the town. Spectacular gardens, including the Jardim Botânico and Quinta do Palheiro, are only a short bus, taxi or cable car ride from the capital.

Small-scale agriculture dominates the island's landscape, and employs about a fifth of its people. Depending on the altitude, and whether you are on the warm south coast or the marginally cooler north coast, you will see terraces of bananas, and the vines that produce the grapes for fortified Madeira wine. There are windswept mountain peaks, craggy cliffs and emerald valleys. From strategically situated lookout points *(miradouros)* you can take in these magical panoramas and look down on villages and terraced fields carved out of the mountains.

New roads and tunnels make driving around Madeira faster than before, though the best scenery is reserved for those who follow the hairpin bends of mountain roads and coastal lanes, getting sprayed by waterfalls and constantly stopping to enjoy spectacular vistas. Madeira is even better when explored on foot. The island is heaven for anyone who enjoys being outside, whether your taste tends to gentle walks or hardcore hiking. Madeira's system of irrigation channels, known as *levadas*, carries water down from the mountains on gentle gradients and provides a ready-made system of trails. The canals – more than 2,100km (1,300 miles) of them wrap around the island – have level footpaths running along their entire length. Walkers of all ages and abilities need only find a *levada* to take in some of the finest countryside anywhere. Several of these walks, which are described later in this book (see page 86), are among the highlights of Madeira.

With such rapturous scenery and a climate that is consistently delightful, perhaps it would be unfair to expect nature to have bestowed miles of perfect sands on the island as well. Madeira has few beaches as such, although most coastal villages have swimming pools and sea access, and Calheta and the bay of Machico have artificial beaches with imported golden sand. But if a chair by the pool just can't compare with waves lapping on sand, you will have to follow in the wake of Columbus and dock on the neighbouring island of Porto Santo, a popular day trip. The only other inhabited island in the archipelago, Porto Santo has a 9km (5.5 mile) beach running the length of its south coast, but few other attractions.

While some surely would find the notion of an island holiday with no beach time

Isolated villages

Some of the mountain villages of Madeira are so isolated that they did not begin to receive TV signals until the 1980s.

an unusual prospect indeed, perhaps it isn't such a tragedy that Madeira's shoreline crashes so violently into the ocean. Lack of sand has kept Madeira from becoming as popular as the Canary Islands or Mallorca. If Madeira had sandy beaches and cheap flights from Europe and North America, it would surely not have managed to preserve as much of its environment as it has. Yet tourism is eroding the island in other ways, as traditional farming gives way to a tourism economy, as a result leaving the vertiginous hills untended and the picturesque terraces and *levadas* in a state of decline.

TOURISM AND MADEIRA

For decades, Madeira has attracted a genteel, even anachronistic, form of island tourism. Afternoon tea and a jacket and tie at dinner are still de rigueur at the most elegant hotels. The typical visitor is still older and wealthier than in most holiday destinations, but times have changed – as they have across Portugal, which is no longer the forgotten backwater of Europe. Funchal's enlarged airport, extended motorway and increasing numbers of new hotels testify to local travel-industry ambitions. Today Madeira is being discovered by younger travellers who might indulge in the spas and dining that world-class hotels offer, but are just as likely to seek out more modest accommodation up in the mountains and strap on their boots for serious hiking.

Madeirans, like most Portuguese, are a generally quiet and reserved people. Add to this geographical isolation and the difficulties of a harsh, mostly agricultural existence and you might well expect the islanders to be less than welcoming. Instead, you will find friendly people who, in spite of a year-long tourism season, are refreshingly hospitable. They are proud of the scenic beauty, delectable wines and exquisite hand embroidery for which their tiny island has rightly become famous.

HISTORY AND CULTURE

As befits a lush, tropical island stranded in the middle of the ocean, Madeira's origins are shrouded in fanciful and imaginative legend. Some claim that the archipelago is all that remains of Plato's lost Atlantis, or that it is part of a landmass that once fused the continents of Europe and America. Recorded history begins in relatively recent times; in the early fifteenth century, just as the golden age of Portuguese discovery was erupting. Under the direction of Henry the Navigator (Henrique o Navegador), caravels set out from the westernmost point of the Algarve, in southern Portugal, in search of foreign lands, fame and wealth. João Gonçalves Zarco, sailing in the service of Prince Henry, made the first of many famous Portuguese discoveries: in 1418 he happened upon a small volcanic archipelago 1,000km (620 miles) from Lisbon.

Perhaps Zarco knew precisely where he was heading, having learned of the existence of Madeira from a Castilian source. After all, the waters of the Canary Islands, only 445km (275 miles) to the south, had supported busy shipping lanes for very nearly a century, and Genovese maps from the mid-fourteenth century depict both Madeira and Porto Santo.

More likely, Zarco was heading for Guinea and storms forced him onto the beach of Porto Santo. If so, then he was fortunate, for he managed to land on the only large, sandy beach for hundreds of miles around.

PORTUGAL'S FIRST COLONY

The following year Zarco returned to claim the larger island he had seen from Porto Santo, and with him went Tristão Vaz Teixeira and Bartolomeu Perestrelo. They officially became the first men to set foot on the heavily forested island, naming it *Ilha da Madeira* – Island of Timber.

The Portuguese Crown, delighted with its first important discovery, embarked on a programme of colonisation. In 1425, King João I pronounced Madeira an official province of Portugal, and presented it as a gift to Prince Henry (Infante Dom Henrique). He, in turn, confirmed the land ownership rights to Zarco and Teixeira, while Perestrelo was awarded Porto Santo.

Occupation of Madeira began in the early 1420s as a decidedly small-scale project: colonists arrived with only as much as they

THE FIRST MAN ON MADEIRA?

Some say that the first man to set foot on the island was not the Portuguese adventurer João Gonçalves Zarco but a fourteenth-century Englishman named Robert Machim (sometimes written as Machin).

One version of the story is that Machim was a knight at the court of Edward III and sought to marry above his station, to a girl named Anne d'Arfet (or Anne of Hertford). The determined young lovers boarded a ship bound for France, which was thrown severely off course. The pair ended up shipwrecked on Madeira. Anne died of exposure soon afterwards, and Machim buried her by the bay where they had come ashore. When Machim died (it is said of a broken heart), the surviving crew buried him alongside her. The crew lived to recount the tragic tale, they eventually escaped the island on a log raft.

Zarco, who is much more widely credited with the discovery of Madeira, was aware of the legend. He is said to have found the grave of the couple, naming the site Machico in honour of Machin. The couple's resting place is said to be beneath the Capela dos Milagres on the eastern side of Machico Bay (see page 64).

Henry the Navigator

could carry from Portugal. They found plenty of water pouring down from the mountains, and more timber than anyone knew what to do with. They set about clearing the land for agriculture, setting fire to tracts of forest. Legend says that a great fire burned for seven years on the island.

ENERGETIC AGRICULTURE

The fire provided the soil with a rich ash fertiliser, which complemented the luxuriant growing conditions of tropical sun and plentiful water. The Portuguese saw valuable economic opportunity in their new possession and sent for Malvasia grapes from Crete and sugar cane from Sicily in an effort to seed the island's first cash crops. The project was not a simple one. Colonists had to find enough level ground to grow crops on, and then solve the issue of irrigating them. Brute strength, without the aid of machinery, carved flat surfaces out of the mountains, and settlers built the terraces that are seen today on the steep slopes.

The problem of watering crops was solved by the irrigation system known as *levadas* – simply designed water channels that wound down from water sources on the verdant mountain tops. The *levadas* were largely built by enslaved labourers from Africa, whose primary employment was on sugar plantations. Madeirans traded sugar, the era's dominant luxury item, with Venice and Flanders, and proved skilful in the art of wine-making. The island's burgeoning economic significance propelled population growth, and by the middle of the fifteenth century Madeira was home to some 800 families. A census in 1514 recorded 5,000 inhabitants, not including enslaved people.

In 1478, Madeira welcomed a visitor who would greatly assist the island's future wine trade. Christopher Columbus, not yet a sailor of any renown, sailed to Madeira on an assignment to buy sugar cane. His sojourn was unsuccessful, as money failed to arrive for part of the shipment. Yet Columbus (Cristóvão Colombo in Portuguese) returned six years later, by which time evidence suggests he had become an experienced sugar merchant. His later discovery of the New World brought prosperity to the Madeiran economy: the island's strategic location on the great East–West trading route meant that ships anchored and took on food, water and the valuable trading commodity of Madeira wine.

Columbus married Dona Filipa Moniz Perestrelo, who was the granddaughter of Porto Santo's first governor, and who fathered a son on the island. Even today, there are people on Porto Santo who will tell you that it was during the time he spent there that Columbus learned navigation techniques, and also found the inspiration to undertake his voyage which took place in 1492.

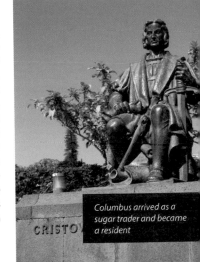

Columbus arrived as a
sugar trader and became
a resident

CRISTOV

First inhabitants

It seems certain that Madeira had never been inhabited before the Portuguese arrived in the fifteenth century. The first settlers found no Stone Age natives, as the Spanish had found in the Canary Islands, and no mysterious monuments to the past, as in the Balearics.

PLUNDERED BY PIRATES

From early in the sixteenth century, Madeira became the target of pirate attacks. Noticing the island's wealth and repository of supplies, buccaneers from Morocco, Algeria and France invaded coastal settlements, plundered villages and left behind a trail of death and destruction. In the year of 1566, Madeira suffered its worst disaster when the French pirate Bertrand de Montluc sailed into Funchal harbour with his 11-galleon armada and 1,300 men. He unleashed a 16-day reign of terror which consequently left 300 Madeirans dead, stocks of sugar destroyed and as a result the island plundered.

As a result of the attack, Porto Santo, which had also been scourged by these villains of the seas, went on to build hilltop beacons to serve as early-warning systems.

On the mainland, an invasion of even greater significance ensued in 1580, when Felipe II of Spain proclaimed himself king of Portugal and marched his armies across the border. The Spanish remained for another 60 years, during which time Madeira was a Spanish territory.

At the end of the sixteenth century, Madeira surrendered its domination of the sugar-cane industry to another, much larger, Portuguese colony: Brazil. Sugar cane had taken a hefty toll on the Madeiran soil and the exhausted plantation soils were supplanted by less demanding grape vines.

MADEIRA AND BRITAIN

Britain's political and economic connections to Madeira can be traced to the seventeenth century. In 1662, Charles II married Portugal's Catherine of Bragança, and a provision written into the bride's dowry granted special favours to British settlers on Madeira. Both Madeira and Britain benefited from a new regulation that governed the shipment of Madeira wine and made it the only wine that could be exported directly to the British possessions in the Western hemisphere. Such trading rights attracted more Britons to the island, who founded dynastic families who, in some cases, still constitute the island's economic elite. Wine profits were huge, and by 1800 exports had reached 9-million bottles per year. Many of the grand country *quintas* (villas) that still dot the island today have their roots in the early Madeira wine industry.

Looe Rock and Funchal in the early nineteenth century

Pirate treasure

The notorious English pirate Captain Kidd was hanged in London after terrorising the high seas for almost a decade – but the loot he amassed was never found. Legend has it that his treasure is buried somewhere on the Ilhas Desertas, southeast of Madeira, although all searches so far have been fruitless.

British troops arrived on the island in 1801 to protect against possible invasion by the French, but they were withdrawn following the Treaty of Amiens in 1802. In 1807, the treaty was put in jeopardy and the troops returned, remaining until 1814. After the fall of Napoleon, many of the garrison remained and settled permanently on the island.

In Madeira, the second half of the nineteenth century was plagued by natural disaster. In 1852, the island's precious vines were blighted by mildew, wiping out an estimated 90 percent of the total crop. Just four years later, cholera claimed the lives of up to 7,000 Madeirans, and in 1872–3 the dreaded phylloxera louse destroyed the remainder of the vineyards. Potato and sugar crops were also badly affected.

Portugal took up arms during World War I, siding with the British and French. Madeira's strategic position for Atlantic shipping did not escape the notice of the German High Command, and in 1916 a German submarine bombarded Funchal harbour and sank three French ships.

MODERN TIMES

As mainland Portugal lurched into a political and economic crisis that would bring down the country's republican government, many miles away Madeira was busy developing its tourist trade: the island had been a sought-after destination since the mid-nineteenth century, attracting wealthy British sun-lovers, minor royalty and aristocrats from many countries. The celebrated Reid's Hotel opened its doors in 1890, and a seaplane service started operating from Southampton in 1921. Madeira was awarded further cachet when the last of the Austro-Hungarian emperors, Charles I of Austria (also Charles IV of Hungary), chose Madeira as his home in exile after World War I. He died here in 1922 and his last resting place, in Monte's Nossa Senhora church, now receives a stream of pilgrims, following his beatification by Pope John Paul II in 2004.

In 1932, Portugal gained a new ruler, Dr António Salazar. His success at controlling inflation and reducing national debt made him a popular hero, but under the new ultra-conservative constitution of 1933 he effectively became dictator for life. Following a bloodless military coup in 1974, Salazar's successor, Dr Marcelo Caetano, was overthrown and free elections were held. Two years later,

CELEBRATED STOPOVERS

Madeira, with its long tradition of hospitality, has welcomed many notable voyagers, including, in 1815, the defeated Napoleon Bonaparte. En route to exile on St Helena in the South Atlantic, Napoleon's ship anchored to take on supplies. The only visitor allowed aboard was the British consul, who graciously presented Britain's old enemy with bottles of vintage Madeira wine to help wile away his confinement – Napoleon responded with gold coins. History just about repeated itself after the 1974 coup, when the deposed Portuguese leaders, ex-President Tomás and Prime Minister Caetano, also stopped at Madeira en route to exile in Brazil. This time the defeated party was allowed ashore, but hospitality was less in evidence, and they were locked up in the São Lourenço fortress.

Madeira was granted the status of Autonomous Political Region. A new island parliament would henceforth deal with all issues directly affecting Madeira, except defence, foreign affairs and tax, and for the first time Madeira was allowed to elect five members to the parliament in Lisbon.

In 1986, Portugal joined the European Economic Community (now the European Union). Generous funding from the EU has been invested in the island's fishing industry and infrastructure, such as roads, tunnels, marinas, leisure complexes and an expanded Funchal airport. When the EU money dried up, President Alberto João Jardim turned to private investors to continue the building boom and in 2012, the tiny island found itself €6 billion in debt.

In 2016, the island was ravaged by wildfires that caused widespread devastation. Following the worst summer heatwave in history, flames destroyed 22 percent of Funchal. Hundreds were forced to abandon their homes and three people were killed.

Between 2020 and 2021, tourism in Madeira stalled due to measures taken to contain the Covid-19 pandemic but with a successful vaccine rollout, entry restrictions have been withdrawn and visitors are gradually returning.

Madeira appeals to tourists in a 1931 poster

IMPORTANT DATES

1351 A Genoese map depicts Madeira for the first time.

1418 Portuguese explorers discover Porto Santo.

1425 Madeira becomes a province of Portugal; sugar cultivation begins, followed by grapes and grain.

1478 Christopher Columbus briefly settles on the island.

1480 Settlers arrive from Europe, including merchants who invest in the sugar plantations and irrigation systems.

1514 The population reaches 5,000. Funchal cathedral completed.

1566 Funchal sacked by French pirates; 300 islanders killed.

1580 Felipe II of Spain occupies Portugal; Madeira falls under Spanish rule.

1640 The Portuguese regain their kingdom (and Madeira).

1703 Britain is granted valuable trade concessions with Portugal. Many Britons settle in Madeira and soon dominate the wine trade.

1801–14 Napoleon occupies Portugal; British troops stationed on Madeira.

1850 European intellectuals and aristocrats 'discover' Madeira.

1872–3 Phylloxera destroys most of Madeira's vines. Bananas replace wine as the island's main cash crop.

1914–18 Portugal fights with the Allies in World War I.

1933 Salazar founds the Estado Novo and becomes dictator of Portugal.

1939–45 Portugal remains neutral in World War II.

1960 Madeira's first airport on Porto Santo opens.

1974 Bloodless revolution overthrows the dictatorship in Portugal.

1976 Madeira becomes an autonomous region with its own parliament.

1986 Portugal joins the EEC; gets funds to improve Madeira's infrastructure.

1989 The first stretch of the Via Rápida motorway opens.

2010 Flash floods cause a mud slide that kills 40 people.

2012 Madeira's debts are estimated at €6 billion.

2015 Miguel Albuquerque becomes the new president of Madeira; Madeira wins title of the World's Leading Island Destination.

2016 Wild fires ravage the island, killing three and destroying 150 homes.

2020 The Covid-19 pandemic hits Madeira.

2022 Restrictions are eased and the economy begins to recover.

The mighty headland of Cabo Girão, on the western coast

OUT AND ABOUT

GETTING AROUND

Madeira's size can be deceptive. At first glance it might seem that two days would be sufficient to see the whole 57 by 22km (35 by 13 miles). Indeed, it is possible to speed from Funchal to once-remote Porto Moniz in under an hour. But to do so means travelling mainly in tunnels. For a taste of the island's beautiful scenery, there is no alternative but to take to Madeira's mountainous terrain and winding, two-lane roads.

A minimum of three days is necessary to see a good portion of the island; a full week allows you to do it justice and take the time to enjoy its scenic outdoors at a relaxed pace. Many visitors are still advised to hop aboard day-trip buses that take in the main attractions: although the roads have improved, travelling by car should only be undertaken by confident drivers who are comfortable negotiating steep, winding terrain.

More and more visitors are choosing to stay outside Funchal; accommodation in mountain lodges and smaller coastal hotels has greatly improved over the years, and there are now visitors who barely set foot in the capital.

FUNCHAL

Funchal ① is the only town of any size on the island – indeed in the whole of the archipelago – and most of Madeira's historic buildings, museums and sights are located in the capital. With a population of around 112,000, it is a larger city than most expect to find on such a tiny island, but you can walk across the centre in just 10 to 15 minutes. Exploring inland to the north is difficult on foot, the streets become very steep. Nevertheless, walking remains the only practical way to see Funchal. The narrow, cobbled streets were never meant for vehicles, and they can be surprisingly congested with traffic, although some have now been pedestrianised.

One way to get your bearings upon arrival in Funchal is to walk out on the jetty known as the **Ilhéu de Pontinha** and view the city as those aboard cruise ships do. The Pontinha, which was built in 1962, leads round the container port and passes the old fortress, which is perched on top of what was once a tiny island known as Looe Rock.

Funchal's deep natural harbour propelled the city's development in the fifteenth and sixteenth centuries, when Madeira became known to those making expeditions to the Far East and the Americas. The busy port hosts cruise ships, yachts and picturesque (and functioning) fishing boats. The commercial freight port of Caniçal is about 12 miles east of Funchal.

THE TOWN CENTRE

The view of the town from the harbour is outstanding: squat white houses with terracotta roofs climb steeply through tropical greenery all around the spacious bay, with rugged mountains forming an attractive backdrop. The dominant building on the seafront is the **Palácio de São Lourenço**

Funchal and its harbour

Palácio de São Lourenço

(Fortress of St Lawrence; Mon 12.30pm, Tues & Wed 10am, Thurs 10am & 12.30pm, Fri 3pm; free tours). Erected in the sixteenth century, it guarded the bay against pirates – you can see the ancient cannons poking through the crenellated walls. Walking up Avenida Zarco, past the main gate of the fort, you will see the white-gloved sentries who guard what is now the residence of Madeira's prime minister and the military command.

At the junction of Avenida Zarco and the main street, Avenida Arriaga, stands Francisco Franco's 1927 statue of Madeira's discoverer, João Gonçalves Zarco, often referred to as the 'First Captain'. Franco's work can be seen all over the city and at the **Museu Henrique e Francisco Franco** (Rua João de Deus 13; Mon–Fri 9am–5.30pm). The imposing **Palácio do Governo Regional Ⓐ**, a handsome building with tiled patios and the administrative headquarters of Madeira, rises behind the Zarco monument to the right. Avenida Arriaga is particularly pretty in late spring, when the jacaranda trees are in full blossom.

Along here you will find the **tourist information office** and, next door at No. 28, the **Adegas de São Francisco** (Blandy's Wine Lodge; www.blandyswinelodge.com; English tours Mon–Fri 10.30am, 2.30pm, 3.30pm, 4.30pm, Sat 10.30am), Madeira's oldest working wine lodge. This atmospheric place was part of a

Franciscan monastery, built in the seventeenth century. Here you can take a tour of the lodge to learn about the wine-making process, and visit the attics where fragrant wines mature in huge oak barrels. You don't need to take a tour to visit the handsome tasting room, decorated with frescoes painted by the German artist Max Römer, in 1922.

Just a few steps west of the lodge is the small **Jardim de São Francisco** (St Francis' Garden), a delightful urban green space with an open-air café set amid lush tropical vegetation. Across from the park is the **Teatro Municipal** (http://teatro.cm-funchal.pt), a miniature Victorian gem that hosts periodic concerts, plays and films. Across the road, in the hotel bearing the same name is the chic **Café Ritz** (www.theritzmadeira.com), an elegant café with regular live music. It was once the Chamber of Commerce and has fine

Funchal's Sé (Cathedral) is one of the island's oldest buildings

azulejo (blue and white tile) vignettes that depict scenes from old Madeira.

Towards the centre, at the east end of Avenida Arriaga (at Rua João Tavira) is Funchal's principal landmark, the **Sé B** (Cathedral; Mon–Fri 7.15am–6.30pm, Sat 8am–noon & 4–7pm, Sun 7.30am–noon & 4.30–7pm;

> ### Jesuit legacy
>
> The building that houses the University of Madeira, to the north of the Praça do Município, was formerly a Jesuit College that also served as a barracks for British troops during the nineteenth century.

free). Begun in 1493 and completed in 1517, the cathedral is one of the few buildings in Funchal to survive from the early days of colonisation. The exterior is plain and simple, topped by a granite clock tower, but the cathedral's interior is lavish and impressive, lined with spectacular decoration. It has Gothic arches, a splendid inlaid cedar ceiling of Moorish design, beautifully carved blue and gold choir stalls, gilded altars and a sprinkling of nice *azulejos*.

Walking up Rua João Tavira, north of the cathedral, note the black and white mosaics paving the pedestrian shopping street, and explore the pretty narrow shopping streets to the right. At the top of Rua João Tavira is **Praça do Município C**, the town's dignified main square, with a huge fish-scale mosaic of black and white stones which gives the impression of an enormous chessboard, and historic buildings on all sides. On the northern side is the seventeenth-century **Igreja de São João Evangelista do Colégio** (Collegiate Church; Mon 11am–6pm, Tues–Fri 10am–6pm, Sat 3–6pm, Sun 9am–1pm & 6.30–8.30pm; free), originally founded by the Jesuits in 1574. A spacious and airy old place, it is decorated with seventeenth- and eighteenth-century tiles, paintings and gilt woodcarving.

At the head of the square (east) stands the **Câmara Municipal** (Town Hall; guided tours Mon–Fri 9am & 5pm), which occupies a

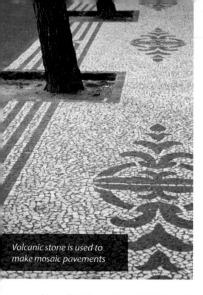

Volcanic stone is used to make mosaic pavements

former eighteenth-century palace. Don't miss the graceful, nineteenth-century statue of *Leda and the Swan* in the inner courtyard. The statue used to be located in the old fish market – a fact that is corroborated by the tiled panel outside the present municipal market (see page 35).

Situated on the square's south side is the **Museu de Arte Sacra D** (Museum of Religious Art; www.museuartesacrafunchal.org; Mon–Fri 10am–5pm, Sat 10am–1pm). The museum is housed in a handsome seventeenth-century palace, the former residence of the bishop of Funchal. The outstanding works on view include a dozen or so fifteenth- and sixteenth-century Flemish paintings, regarded as among the richest in Portugal and rare even in the rest of Europe.

These vibrant masterpieces, as well as other excellent works from the Portuguese school of the same period, were donated to the island's churches by Madeira's wealthy sugar merchants, who during the sixteenth century traded their 'white gold' in Antwerp, which was then the home of a thriving artistic culture. There is also a fine collection of Flemish sculpture, as well as a curation of goldsmithery.

The main door of the museum leads to Rua do Bispo (Bishop Street) and both this and the parallel street, Rua Queimada Cima, are well worth exploring for their shops, cafés and historic buildings.

Continue west from the Praça do Municipio on Rua da Carreira, a bustling street full of popular old-fashioned shops and affordable restaurants. Left of here is the **Museu de Fotografia da Madeira** (www.facebook.com/mfmvicentes; Tues–Sat 10am–5pm) with photographs reflecting 150 years of island life.

Further down the Rua da Carreira is the picturesque Rua da Mouraria, with antiques shops and the **Museu de História Natural** (www.facebook.com/museuhistorianaturalfunchal; Tues–Sun 10am–6pm), another eighteenth-century aristocratic home converted into a museum. On the ground floor is a modest aquarium (closed for restoration until early 2023) showing Madeira's sea life, while upstairs you will find an old-fashioned collection of stuffed local sea and land creatures.

At the top of the street is the charming **Igreja de São Pedro**

(daily 9am–noon & 3–7pm; free), built in the sixteenth century. Its walls are lined entirely with blue and white check-patterned *azulejos* and it has a beautifully painted wooden ceiling, fine chandeliers, a massive gilded altar and side chapels.

About halfway up the steep Calçada de Santa Clara, at No. 7, you reach the **Casa Museu Frederico de Freitas** (Freitas House-Museum; www.facebook.com/cmfredericofreitas; Tues–Sat 10am–5.30pm). It is divided into

Stone Manueline window, Quinta das Cruzes

two parts: the modern wing is dedicated to *azulejos* and their history, while the old mansion alongside, the Casa de Calçada, is full of paintings of Madeira by nineteenth-century artists, and the furnishings of an affluent nineteenth-century household.

Continue uphill to the **Convento de Santa Clara** (Mon–Sat 10am–noon & 3–5pm). Built towards the end of the fifteenth century and expanded two centuries later, it is now a school run by Franciscan nuns, but you can visit the convent and its church by ringing the bell by the convent gate. The church is a splendid building, with walls completely covered by rare seventeenth-century *azulejos* in geometric patterns, and with a fine painted ceiling. The ornate tomb at the back of the church is sometimes mistaken for that of Zarco, the island's discoverer; in fact, it is the tomb of his son-in-law – Zarco's humbler grave lies beneath the modern timber floor of the high altar.

During his stint as governor of the island, Zarco lived a short way up Calçada do Pico, in the **Quinta das Cruzes ⑤** (https://mqc.madeira.gov.pt/en; Tues–Sat 10am–5.30pm; gardens free). Constructed in the fifteenth century, but rebuilt after an earthquake in 1748 and expanded in the nineteenth century, this is Funchal's finest *quinta* (villa) open to the public. The main house is a museum of antiques: superb sixteenth-century Indo-Portuguese and seventeenth-century Madeiran as well as eighteenth- and nineteenth-century English pieces. The house is surrounded by a lovely, somewhat unkempt garden of exotic flowers, trees and plants.

Rua das Cruzes, the road separating Quinta das Cruzes from the convent, leads to a lookout point with a view over the town, the port and the dome of the English Church.

THE MARKET, OLD TOWN AND SEAFRONT

Between two *ribeiras* (river beds) that carry excess water from the mountains to the sea, is Rua Dr Fernão Ornelas, lined with old shops, it leads to Funchal's central market. In spring, the little rivers are hidden beneath trellises of blazing bougainvillea. Directly ahead lies the **Mercado dos Lavradores**  (Workers' Market; http://mercados.cm-funchal.pt; Mon–Fri 7am–7pm, Sat 7am–2pm), housed in a two-storey, open-roofed structure built in 1937. The best time to visit is on Friday or Saturday, when fishermen, farmers and traders from all over the island pour into town. This is the only time when the central part is entirely filled with stalls. The market is bustling, fragrant and colourful, with fruit, vegetables and fish of all shapes, colours and sizes. Meat stalls can be found around the outside, as well as several wicker and handicraft shops.

The market marks the start of the **Zona Velha**  (Old Town). The main streets are the narrow, cobbled alleyway of Rua de Santa Maria and, parallel, Rua Dom Carlos I. Once poor and decaying, but

Stalls at the Mercado dos Lavradores

filled with character, this former fishermen's quarter has been transformed into a focus of tourist interest, with a seafront promenade, a cable-car station taking passengers up to the hill town of Monte (see page 41) and a popular attraction called the **Madeira Story Centre** (www.madeirastorycentre.com; daily 9am–7pm), packed with exhibits, videos and interactive displays recounting the history of the island.

The main focus of gentrification is the row of restaurants you reach at the pedestrian-only stretch at the eastern end, beyond which lies the **Capela do Corpo Santo** (Chapel of the Body of Christ; Mon–Fri 9.30am–12.30pm & 2–6pm; free). The chapel, dating from the end of the fifteenth century, is one of the oldest in Funchal, built by a charity supporting the local fishermen. The low houses beyond once housed fishing families, but are gradually being taken over

The view from the Fortaleza de São Tiago

by artisans making leather
sandals or selling lace and
embroidery.

At the far end of the Old
Town is the **Fortaleza de
São Tiago** (tel: 291 213 340;
St James's Fortress; Mon–Fri
9.30am–5.30pm, free). Built
in the seventeenth century
and expanded in the middle

> **Niemeyer's work**
>
> The architect of the striking
> Pestana Casino Park hotel
> was the Brazilian, Oscar
> Niemeyer. He also designed
> the adjoining casino, which
> is built in the shape of a
> giant crown of thorns.

of the eighteenth, the picturesque fort now houses an excellent
restaurant with views along the steep cliffs that rise to the east
of Funchal.

Back on the seafront, heading west, is the **Assembleia
Regional**, the Regional Parliament, with a modern debating
chamber located in the **Alfândega Velha** (Old Customs House),
built in the sixteenth century and later converted to house the
assembly. Two blocks west, on Praça do Colombo, the **Museu a
Cidade do Açúcar** (City of Sugar Museum; www.facebook.com/
MuseuCidadedoAcucar; Mon–Fri 9am–5.30pm) tells the story of
the island's fifteenth-century sugar trade.

WEST OF TOWN

Avenida Arriaga ends at the Praça do Infante, where a statue of
Prince Henry the Navigator sits at the easternmost tip of **Parque
Santa Catarina** ⓗ (St Catherine's Park; daily April–Sept 7am–9pm,
Oct–March 8am–7pm; free). A delightful hilltop retreat, this park
has splendid views over the marina. Aside from the gardens, lake
and playground, other points of interest include a collection of
bronze statues (including *The Sower* by Francisco Franco, which
dates from 1923); and the Chapel of Santa Catarina from 1425,
said to be the island's oldest chapel. At the west end of the park,

the elegant pink **Quinta Vigia** is the residence of the president of Madeira.

Above the park looms the startling sight of the Pestana Casino Park hotel. This giant box of a hotel signals the start of the traditional hotel zone, flush with five-star hotels such as the Royal Savoy, the Pestana Carlton and Belmond Reid's Palace, plus a few *quintas* and posh restaurants. On the waterfront here, the **CR7 Museum** (https://museucr7.com; Mon–Sat 10am–5pm) dedicated to Cristiano Ronaldo, who was born on the island, is a must for all football fans. North of Reid's Palace stands **MAMMA** (Museu de Arte Moderna

CLIFFTOP PALACE

Standing high over Funchal harbour is Reid's, one of the world's most famous hotels. It was begun by William Reid, a Scot who arrived in Madeira aged 14 in 1836, having run away to sea. He became a prosperous wine merchant in Funchal and by the age of 25 was also renting and managing *quintas* for well-to-do invalids from northern Europe. He converted some of the villas into hotels, and in due course acquired the clifftop site for the luxury hotel of his dreams. He died before it could be finished, and the project was completed by his sons Willy and Albert. Reid's finally opened its doors in 1891. In 1937, the hotel passed into the hands of the Blandy family, another famous British-Madeiran dynasty, and in 1996, it was acquired by the Orient-Express group, which has refurbished it without sacrificing any of its fin de siècle grandeur, and restored its original name, Reid's Palace (although now prefixed by Belmond). It remains the epitome of upper-class luxury, and eminent guests over the years have included Sir Winston Churchill, Charles I of Austria, General Batista of Cuba, and the writer George Bernard Shaw, who signed up for dancing lessons here at the grand age of 71.

na Madeira; www.facebook.com/MammaArtMuseum; Tues–Sat 10am–6pm, Sun 10am–3pm), this creative and challenging museum opened in 2021. To the west the *Zona Turista* stretches along the clifftops, lined with resort complexes and a seafront promenade featuring swimming pools and cafés.

GLORIOUS GARDENS

A short bus or taxi ride into the hillsides northeast of Funchal (on the road to Camacha) takes you to the wonderful **Jardim Botânico ❶** (Botanical Garden; daily 9am–6pm), the most comprehensive public garden on the island. A wonderland for any plant-lover, the gardens have examples of virtually every plant that grows on Madeira and lots of subtropical flowers and plants from far-flung destinations. It occupies steep terraces that offer fine views over Funchal.

Incorporated into the Botanical Garden, **Jardim dos Loiros** (Bird Park) contains all manner of tropical birds including Australian parakeets and dwarf parrots. Uphill from the Botanical Garden, the **Teleférico do Jardim Botânico** (Botanical Garden Cable Car; www.telefericojardimbotanico.com; daily 9am–5pm) offers the chance to glide high above the green ravine west of the Botanical Garden up to the hill town of Monte (see page 41). It is a fantastic trip.

Orchid lovers may want to head downhill to the **Jardim Orquídea** (Pregetter's Orchid Garden; Rua Pita da Silva, 37; www.facebook.com/Jardim.Orquidea; daily 9am–6pm). Badly damaged by fires in 2016 – more than 50,000 plants were lost – the garden has been painstakingly restored in the intervening period.

The **Quinta da Boa Vista** (Rua Luís Figueiroa de Albuquerque; Mon–Sat 9am–6pm), on the eastern side of the city is also dedicated to orchids. Set in the grounds of a beautiful 200-year-old villa, this is a busy working orchid farm. Founded in the 1960s, it has received numerous awards, most notably from the British Royal Horticultural Society.

Formal gardens at the Jardim Botânico

But the most splendid of Madeira's horticultural wonders are the **Palheiro Gardens ❶** (www.palheironatureestate.com/palheirogardens; daily 9am–5pm). The hillside estate, only a short bus ride from Funchal to the east of the city, is the property of the family that once owned Reid's Hotel (see page 38) and is one of the famous producers of Madeira wine. Built in the 1820s, the *quinta* has been in the hands of the Blandy family for more than a century. The gardens are styled rather like an English country garden, and are famous for their winter-flowering camellias. The long, cobbled entrance avenue is shaded by plane trees, while the fields that lie on either side are carpeted with a wonderful spread of arum and belladonna lilies in spring, and agapanthus in summer and autumn.

Formal and informal areas are landscaped with pools and fountains, while terraces tumble down the hillsides. A deep, wild ravine with thick tropical vegetation is nicknamed the 'Valley of Hell'. Yet the garden retains the distinctive, charming and peaceful atmosphere of the timeless grounds of an English country house.

AROUND FUNCHAL

A number of excellent visits are within easy reach of Funchal, so be sure to make the most of its surroundings. Tour operators often promote Monte, Camacha and Curral das Freiras as popular half-day excursions.

MONTE

The hilltop town of **Monte** ❷ has been fashionable ever since wealthy merchants and exiled aristocrats in the nineteenth century built their splendid *quintas* up here in the cool air above

DOWNHILL RACERS

Monte's famous wicker toboggans were used at the beginning of the nineteenth century to carry freight down the frighteningly steep 5km (3-mile) hill between Monte and Funchal. A British merchant, living in Monte and weary of winding his way down to Funchal every day, hit on the idea that the same toboggans could carry people. A wicker seat was fixed to the basic sled and so the *carros de cesto* (literally basket-cars) were born. Each *carro* is controlled by two *carreiros*, complete with traditional straw boaters, who give an initial push and then ride along until another push, or pull, or sudden brake, is required, depending on the desired speed and any traffic ahead. For brakes they use the rubber soles of their boots.

The modern toboggan ride (www.carreirosdomonte.com; Mon–Sat 9am–6pm, last departure from Monte 5.45pm) is but a pale shadow of its former self (even though the fare of €25 for one person, €30 for two, €45 for three, is worthy of a high-tech roller-coaster). The road surface is no longer the friction-free, slippery cobbles that once had *carros* careering down the hill. Toboggans now slide more slowly than they used to. The lot of the *carreiros* has also improved, even if their outfits remain traditional. They used to have to walk back up the hill, carrying or pushing the 68kg (150lb) sleds, but nowadays they make the journey by truck.

The luxuriant Palheiro Gardens

Funchal. Today, it is perhaps best known for the hair-raising toboggan rides that originate here, though the toboggans now have a more modern rival in the form of the cable cars that link Monte with the Jardim Botânico (see page 39) and to Funchal's Old Town (Teleférico da Madeira; www.telefericodofunchal. com; daily 9am–5.45pm).

Monte's main square can be found on the western side of the town, and is a pleasant evocation of yesteryear. The rattling rack-and-pinion railway that once laboured up the ferociously steep hill closed in the 1930s, but the railway station is still here on the western side of the tree-shaded square, and the viaduct arches now rise over the perfectly clipped public gardens of the **Jardim do Monte** (established 1894; free).

A short walk up a path from the square is the elegant and richly decorated **Igreja de Nossa Senhora do Monte** (Our Lady of Monte), dedicated to Madeira's patron saint. On the Feast of the Assumption, 15 August, thousands make the annual pilgrimage to the church. Others come throughout the year to pray at the chapel on the left of the church that holds the tomb of the last of the Austro-Hungarian emperors, Charles I of Austria (and IV of Hungary), who died in Madeira in 1922, and whose path to sainthood was prepared when he was beatified by Pope John Paul II in 2004. At the foot of the church steps is the starting point of the **Carrinhos do Monte** – the ride down the hill aboard a wicker toboggan (see page 41).

The **Jardim do Palácio do Monte** (Monte Palace Tropical Gardens; www.montepalacemadeira.com; daily 9.30am–6pm), a short walk east of the church, is firmly rooted in the past. The gardens that surround the château-like Monte Palace – once the area's most fashionable hotel – are home to hundreds of plants and various other displays. They are lushly beautiful, and within the gates is an impressive collection of native and exotic flora (especially good cycads), a koi pond, a porcelain collection and historical artefacts from throughout Portugal, including architectural pieces taken from important buildings and prized *azulejo* panels. The unimpeded views of Funchal are unbeatable. The **Monte Palace Museum** (daily 10am–4.30pm) houses more

Transport by wicker toboggan

than 1,000 sculptures and a unique mineral collection including beautifully presented precious and semi-precious stones from around the world.

Another garden is that of the villa in which the Emperor Charles I spent the brief months of his exile in Madeira. The **Quinta Jardins do Imperador** (Mon–Fri 9.30am–5.30pm) lies on the western side of the town square, along Caminho do Pico.

Terreiro da Luta, at 876 metres (2,873ft), has its base about 1.5km (1 mile) north of Monte, but climbs another 330 metres (1,080ft) to the top and offers another magnificent panorama of Funchal. It was here that the figure of Our Lady of Monte (now in the church below) was allegedly discovered in the fifteenth century. On the summit is a monument to Nossa Senhora da Paz (Our Lady of Peace), dedicated to the end of World War I. Around the monument are anchor chains from French ships sunk in Funchal harbour by German torpedoes.

VILLAGES IN THE HILLS

A good half-day excursion by bus, taxi or organised tour is the 16km (10-mile) trip north on the narrow, twisting road to **Curral das Freiras** ❸ (Refuge of the Nuns), a village that has been isolated from the outside world for the majority of its history, a perfect crater surrounded by extinct volcanoes. The nuns in question fled here from Santa Clara Convent in the sixteenth century to escape raiding pirates. Protected on all sides – hidden would be more accurate – by a wall of inaccessible mountains, and supported by rich volcanic soil and abundant sunshine, their settlement became permanent.

The village became famous for its cherries and chestnuts, and the popular liqueurs made from those products: *ginja* and *licor de castanha*; the cakes here are also excellent. The village continued in splendid isolation until the twentieth century, when tunnels were bored through the mountains to bring the first roads. Television finally reached the village in 1986.

Curral das Freiras is nice enough, but its whitewashed houses with terracotta roofs are best seen from above. The view from the lookout point of **Eira do Serrado** (1,006 metres/3,300ft) is breathtaking. If you opt for a bus tour, make sure a stop at Eira do Serrado is included (there is also great shopping and an *estalagem*, or inn, here). An alternative view is from the south, across the valley, at the lookout point **Boca dos Namorados** (Lovers' Nest). This is a difficult trek, which, although feasible by car, is usually incorporated on Jeep safari itineraries. From here, the panorama sweeps round and takes in the entire valley (though even at 1,100 metres/3,608ft you will still be close enough to hear the bell of the village church).

Curral das Freiras, the Refuge of the Nuns

In the opposite direction, 16km (10 miles) northeast of Funchal, is **Camacha**, a pretty village at nearly 700 metres (2,300ft). In the heart of willow country, it is the island's centre of the wickerwork industry. Many of the local inhabitants are employed crafting furniture, table mats, baskets and other household items. Around Camacha, and especially to the north of here, you are likely to see the stripped willow soaked and left to dry, either by a riverbank, propped up against a house, or in wigwam fashion in the fields. You may even see families at the roadside, soaking the willow in vats and stripping off the bark. If you look around, you will find lots of cultural, social and entertainment events. One of the best examples is the local folklore groups, they are well-known throughout the world. The village is also notable for its Apple Festival.

Camacha is the starting point for two excellent *levada* walks heading west to Vale do Paraíso and northeast to Eira de Fora. To enjoy these walks without getting lost, you need a walking guidebook, such as Sunflower Books' ultra-reliable *Walk & Eat Madeira* guide, available in shops all over the island (see page 124).

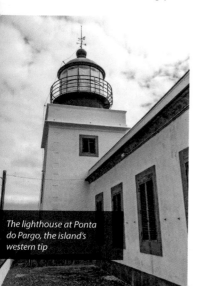

The lighthouse at Ponta do Pargo, the island's western tip

WESTERN MADEIRA

Western Madeira begins just beyond the capital's tourist zone. Here, the pace is slower and the coast even

Picturesque Câmara de Lobos is still an active fishing village

less discovered than further east. Inland offers some glorious countryside.

CÂMARA DE LOBOS AND CABO GIRÃO

Situated just 8.5km (5.3 miles) west of Funchal is **Câmara de Lobos** ❹ (Lair of the Sea-wolves). The peculiar name refers to the seals that once swam near here. Câmara de Lobos is more picturesque from afar than it is up close. In 1950, Winston Churchill spent time on the island painting the fishing port, an interest that ensured its standing as an idyllic, old-world fishing village. The gaily painted boats are still here bobbing in the water, as is the protected, natural rocky harbour.

The port area has resisted attempts at gentrification and fairly swaggers with macho atmosphere. Hard-drinking locals down *poncha* (sugar-cane brandy, lemon juice and honey) in shadowy bars, while grizzled old fishermen play cards or repair their boats.

Close to the waterfront is the small Fishermen's Chapel, an early fifteenth-century project that was later rebuilt (1723), and where locals give thanks for the villagers' safe return from the sea. The regenerated islet of Câmara de Lobos, a cliff (resembling an island) where most fishermen live, is now a venue of cultural activities and has a beautiful garden with stunning views which look over the sea.

Beyond Câmara de Lobos, the coastal road climbs for 8km (5 miles), also dipping inland, passing through rich agricultural country, famous for the high quality of its grapes. Eventually it leads to the top of the mighty headland known as **Cabo Girão** ❺. One of the highest cliffs in the world, it plummets 590 metres (1,900ft) to the Atlantic. The views east and west along the coast are sensational.

There's a terrifying, exhilarating viewpoint, where you stand on a glass floor, clutching a glass-panelled rail, with nothing else beneath you save the sweep of the wild sea hundreds of metres below. Agapanthus cling to the top of the promontory, and pine and eucalyptus creep right to the edge, but an even greater degree of daring can be seen hundreds of metres below, where farmers have managed to salvage tiny plots of arable land, terracing them on the sides and base of the cliff.

The winding road continues on through the sprawling settlements of Quinta Grande and Campanário. The latter, an important grape-growing area, is also remarkable for its cliff-side caves, used by local fishermen for storage purposes.

RIBEIRA BRAVA

The next major settlement, heading west, is **Ribeira Brava** ❻. If you are in a hurry, it can be reached in just 20 minutes on the *Via Rápida* from Funchal. The town's name, which means 'wild river' or 'wild ravine', seems hyperbolic for such an orderly and peaceful little community. Except in winter, Ribeira Brava's river is more of a tame trickle. The river heads due north, as does the road – straight across the island (a mere 20km/12 miles) to São Vicente – making the ancient town of Ribeira Brava (established in 1440) an important junction.

The main focus of attention here is the ornate, sixteenth-century **São Bento** (St Benedict's church), adorned with some of the island's finest gilded and carved woodwork, a nativity and an elaborate font. In Rua de São Francisco, the fascinating **Museu Etnográfico da Madeira** (Madeira Ethnographic Museum; tel: 291 952 598; Tues–Fri 9.30am–5pm, Sat 10am–12.30pm & 1.30–5.30pm) is an excellent introduction to the fishing, farming and wine-making traditions that still just about survive in Madeira's more remote outposts.

Bananas are big business along the south coast of Madeira

THE SOUTHWEST COAST

From Ribeira Brava, most coach excursions head north to São Vicente (see page 53), as the road cuts through some of the best scenery on the whole island. However, those with more time can continue along the southwest coast.

Ponta do Sol is the next village after Ribeira Brava. As its name suggests, it is blessed with more than its fair share of sunshine. Only during the summer does it really come alive, however, when beach umbrellas are set out on the seafront lido. There are two buildings of note here: an eighteenth-century church and an arts centre, the **John dos Passos Cultural Centre**, (tel: 291 974 034; Mon–Fri 9am–12.30pm & 2–5.30pm; free) housed in the restored home of the American novelist's grandparents, who emigrated from this village in the mid-nineteenth century. The centre hosts temporary exhibitions, seminars and conferences.

About 10km (6 miles) west of Ponta do Sol is **Calheta** ❼, a banana plantation centre and the only town of significance as you head west. The Igreja Matriz, the parish church, dates from 1430 but was rebuilt in 1639, and features a handsome Moorish-style ceiling. Next door is the Engenho da Calheta, a sugar mill, which produces honey and rum. Calheta has been the beneficiary of substantial tourism investment, with a large artificial-sand beach, and the **Museu de Arte Contemporânea** (MUDAS; www.facebook.com/MUDASmuseu; Tues–Sun 10am–5pm), located on the clifftop to the west of the town. Besides a collection of more than 400 works by Portuguese artists, it also houses an auditorium, a library, shop, café and restaurant.

From Calheta, a steep inland road climbs to the very centre of the island, up to the **Paúl da Serra** ❽ (High Moorland). This plateau measures some 17 by 6km (11 by 3.5 miles), and the flat plain stands in dramatic contrast to the rugged mountains elsewhere on Madeira. The scenery is reminiscent of the moors of Scotland, and can be bleak, but on clear days it is possible to see both the north and south coasts of the island. In good weather, hikers are drawn to its remote and barren character. If you are thinking of hiking here, be warned that mists descend suddenly; you may want to go with a guide (see page 119).

Where the road from Calheta joins the main road across the moorland, turn right for the large car park that serves **Rabaçal** ❾, a beautiful valley popular among Madeirans at weekends and holidays. This is the starting point for a couple of spectacular *levada* walks. Both involve walking downhill from the car park along the narrow and twisting tarmac road that leads to the rest house and barbecue pits at Rabaçal, then following the signs. The trip to the **Risco waterfall** is flat and takes about 30 minutes there and back. The other takes about three hours and involves a pretty

Natural swimming pools in the volcanic rock at Porto Moniz

steep climb along the way to **25 Fontes** (25 Springs) – as the name suggests, a verdant and water-filled spot. Both walks, indicated on almost all maps of Madeira, are wonderfully scenic.

THE NORTHWEST COAST

At the island's extreme northwestern tip is **Porto Moniz ⑩**, 75km (46 miles) from Funchal via the coastal road (only 50km/30 miles across the island), but it seems a world away. A tongue of volcanic lava flowed into the Atlantic thousands of years ago; it cooled and was carved by the sea into a series of protected natural pools. Small plots of land, divided by heath-tree fencing (to protect crops from the salt-laden wind) climb the hills overlooking the sea. You could spend a happy hour or two here, especially if the weather is warm and you want to paddle in rock pools or sit on the volcanic rocks and contemplate the ocean. There are several restaurants selling fish and seafood.

East from here, the dramatic **coastal road** is one of the island's star attractions. The original road (signposted Antiga 101 – Old 101), carved into the cliff in 1950, is a one-way route that can only be driven east to west (from São Vicente to Porto Moniz). Driving the other way on the coastal road you will catch a glimpse of this old corniche road, literally set on a ledge cut into the cliff face. As you depart Porto Moniz, you will pass a rocky outcrop with a hole carved into it like an open window; this has lent its name to the nearest settlement, **Ribeira da Janela** (Valley of the Window). After rain, you might also see water gushing down from the mountains and forming waterfalls.

Seixal ⑪ ('say-shall') is the only other settlement before São Vicente. The Sercial grape, used to produce the driest style of Madeira wine, grows on impossible-seeming steep terraces behind this coastal village, protected from wind and salt-laden air by bracken fences.

São Vicente ⑫, perhaps the prettiest village on the island, begins at the point where the northern coastal road meets the north–south road heading 21km (13 miles) to Ribeira Brava. The town lies just south of an unusual little chapel carved out of a rock. São Vicente's compact, well-kept centre is pedestrian-only, and attractive shops and cafés look onto Igreja Matriz, a lovely church with a painted ceiling depicting St Vincent. Tourism is making inroads, and a few restaurants have been designed with day-trippers in mind, but the village remains pristine – it is set inland, protected from the harsh ocean winds.

The **Grutas e Centro do Vulcanismo** (Caves and Volcanology Centre; tel: 291 842 404; www.grutasecentrodovulcanismosaovicente.com; Tues–Sun 9am–6pm) is situated on the opposite side of the river from the village. Formed when a now-extinct volcano

São Vicente, one of Madeira's most attractive villages

Changeable weather

Madeira is known for its microclimates. Even though it's a small island, the weather can change several times over the course of the day, or if you move just 5km (3 miles). Clouds come and go with great alacrity, so don't despair if a day starts overcast – the clouds may clear in a matter of minutes.

erupted more than 400,000 years ago, the caves were carved by molten lava. The extraordinary 'tubes' formed are more than 1km (0.6 miles) in length. In 1855, an Englishman discovered the caves, which, being a lava bed, do not have icy limestone stalagmites and stalactites but instead are adorned with 'lava drops' that look like thick whirls of chocolate mousse. In a low-rise building near the cave entrance is an exhibition centre with some technical displays on volcanic processes and the island's geology, but also some enjoyable audiovisuals showing how Madeira and its neighbouring islands were formed by the combination of volcanic eruption and the erosive effects of wind and rain. For a friendlier environment, head to the Indigenous Garden in the centre of the town which features dozens of species of local flora and makes for a delightful afternoon.

High on a hill above the village is an odd church – actually a clockless clock tower – standing over a small chapel dedicated to Our Lady of Fátima. This isolated spot is a significant pilgrimage site, and can be seen for kilometres around.

From here, the road tunnels through the mountains back to Ribeira Brava, but the old road continues to cut its way upwards through verdant countryside until finally coming to a crest at the pass of **Boca da Encumeada** (626 metres/2,054ft). From here you can see right to the north coast and well into the south, while on each side are vast expanses of mountain scenery. This is one of the starting points for treks to Pico Ruivo, which is the highest peak on the island (1,862 metres/6,109ft).

One of the best *levada* walks on the island skirts the edge of the mountain and takes in the entire valley, with views of the sea. Look for the steps opposite the Bar-Restaurant Boca da Encumeada. The walk along the irrigation canal is lined with hydrangeas and ferns. It's around a 45-minute walk until you reach a second tunnel. From here you can return to follow Levada das Rabaças for more amazing views.

About 3km (1.5 miles) south of the pass, perched on the edge of Serra de Água, is a handsome mountain chalet, the best of its kind on Madeira – the **Pousada dos Vinháticos** (a *vinhático* is a type of Madeiran mahogany tree) with fabulous mountain views. Up until 2021, the building was celebrated as the only surviving pousada

Mountains near Pico de Arieiro

on the island and the perfect place for lunch on the terrace, but sadly it too has had to close its doors to visitors.

The valley on the opposite side of the road, south of the *pousada*, is known as **Serra de Água** and was the island's first hydro-electric power station (Madeira now has four). In spite of the modern technology, the valley remains a quiet agricultural community tucked away in some of the island's lushest hills.

The road from here leads down into Ribeira Brava, where the *Via Rápida* motorway whisks you back to Funchal.

THE CENTRAL HIGHLANDS

The rugged mountain range that splits the island into north and south makes weather forecasting difficult in Madeira. While it is usually warm and clear down in Funchal, the mountains are often shrouded in a wintry mist. But this doesn't necessarily mean that you will have no view once you start climbing. You'll often catch a glimpse of mountain tops jutting through the clouds, a spectacular sight in itself. Madeira's microclimates are hard to judge, however, especially from below. If it looks like a clear day, beat a hasty path up to Pico do Arieiro first thing in the morning. By the time you get to Poiso you should know whether the journey will be worth the effort.

To see a particularly picturesque section of this terrain, drive north (and uphill) from Funchal towards Santana on the north coast on the ER103. There are beautiful vistas, secluded villages and a range of exhilarating walks en route.

PICO DO ARIEIRO

At 1,818 metres (5,900ft), **Pico do Arieiro** ⓭ is Madeira's third-highest mountain, and its summit is reachable by car. As the road rises, the rugged countryside becomes spectacularly barren, though plunging volcanic hillsides have been softened and greened by time.

The lookout point at the windswept, Mars-like summit provides a 360-degree panorama. With its stratified canyon walls, a field of frozen lava and rust-red boulders, it's a geologist's dream. During summer, the terrain is parched, while at other times it is often covered with snow. The overnight temperature plunges below freezing most of the year, while the average annual temperature is below 10°C (50°F). There is also six times as much rain here as in Funchal. If the arrival of clouds catches you unaware, take refuge in the café on the summit.

At 1,862 metres (6,109ft), **Pico Ruivo**, the 'rooftop of Madeira', is only fractionally higher than Pico do Arieiro, but stands as being much less accessible. The peak can be reached by a walk

Climbers reach the summit of Pico Ruivo

of approximately one hour from Achada do Teixeira in the north, or the classic but strenuous four-hour round-trip hike from Pico do Arieiro. The latter is well signposted and there is a paved footpath, with drops protected by railings. The trek is a popular activity; on a good day you will see several other walkers here, so don't worry about losing your way. Warm clothing and hiking boots are essential here, though, and during the winter season bear in mind that conditions on the mountains can be hazardous, with landslides removing parts of the path as well as icy winds and slippery mud. If you suffer from vertigo it is best not to even attempt the walk.

RIBEIRO FRIO AND THE LEVADA TRAILS

Back on the main road north (past Poiso) is the enchanting **Ribeiro Frio** ⑭, more a bend in the road than a town. Though the name means Cold River, it is a sunny and sheltered spot. If it happens to be cold or wet, pop into Restaurante Ribeiro Frio, which resembles an Alpine chalet, warming visitors with log fires and freshly grilled trout from the hatchery across the road. You may have to wait to be served, as it's a very popular choice. Adjacent to the restaurant is a tiny chapel and a small botanical garden.

The trout hatchery is a series of interconnected

Following a levada trail

concrete pools; the trout become increasingly large as you go along them. The botanical garden is not in the same league as the beautiful gardens in Funchal, but it nevertheless claims to have examples of every native species of flower, plant and tree to be found in Madeira, and sprawls unpredictably along twisting paths among shady trees.

Ribeiro Frio is relaxing, but its popularity is due to the two **walks** that begin here. The shorter one covers 2km (1 mile) to the outstanding lookout point known as the **Balcões** (Balconies), and takes just 45 minutes there and back. After a stroll through the woods, you reach a series of platforms that seem suspended in mid-air, with stupendous views across steep hillsides and dramatic ravines to the distinctive peaks of Ruivo and Arieiro. If it's not hidden in cloud cover, the sight certainly ranks as one of the most beautiful on the island. The second walk is one of the island's most popular *levada* trails (see page 119). This circular walk continues for around 7km (4.3 miles). Follow the signs for Portela and then walk along the Levada do Furado, turning right along the Levada do Bezerro. You will then cross the plateau Chão das Feiteiras before returning to Ribeiro Frio. An alternative, longer walk is to continue on the Levada do Furado until it reaches **Portela**. This walk takes most people about three hours, so you may wish to arrange for a taxi to collect you at Portela.

THE ROAD TO SANTANA

North of Ribeiro Frio, towards the coast, is **Faial**, set picturesquely at the foot of the Penha d'Águia (Eagle Rock). There is little of note in the village itself, aside from a handsome church and the Casa de Chá do Faial (Faial Tea Room) – actually a restaurant, with picture windows and fine rooftop panoramas. The road winds west past several good lookout points for fine views of the village from the main road.

Santana ⑮ is home to an enchantingly picture-book style of housing – A-framed structures known as *palheiros* (very similar to the A-framed cow huts that dot the hillsides around the town). The classic *palheiro* is a two-storey white stucco house with a brightly painted red door, red and blue window-frames and shutters and, essentially, a thatched roof. Two *palheiros*, perfectly painted in red, white and blue, are the objects of many tourist cameras because they are located in the centre of the village (one houses a tourist information centre).

Another *palheiro* that you can explore is in the grounds of the north **Parque Temático do Madeira** (Madeira Theme Park; www. parquetematicodamadeira.pt; Tues–Sun April–Oct 10am–7pm, Nov & Dec until 6pm, Jan–March until 3pm). Set in three hectares (seven acres) of land, this is one of Madeira's best attractions for

LEVADA TRAILS

Few man-made things on Madeira can rival its natural gifts. *Levadas* – simple irrigation channels that provide direct access to the best of the island's natural beauty – offer the best of both worlds. Cut no more than 50cm (20 in) wide, and set 30–60cm (1–2ft) into the ground, *levadas* run more than 2,100km (1,300 miles) around Madeira and have been here almost as long as the island has been settled. The footpaths alongside each *levada* were built for maintenance purposes, but they create a great network for exploring the interior of the island. Some *levadas* are suitable for people of all ages; the only requirements are reasonable footwear and a reliable guidebook (Sunflower Books), see page 124) and, perhaps, a taxi waiting at the other end. As *levadas* wind through the hillsides, most gradients are gentle, but paths that follow the lie of the hillside can also give rise to unexpected vertiginous drops.

Santana's unusual palheiros are unique to the area

children, with rock-climbing walls, adventure playgrounds and a boating lake, plus some good displays on the ecology, history, customs and landscape of the Madeiran islands.

Thatched houses of a larger, more conventional kind are to be found 5km (3 miles) south of Santana, in **Queimadas**, a complex of cottage-style rest houses with attractive gardens, set in the midst of a UNESCO-listed forest. It's a lovely spot for a picnic, although if the weather is clear you might take the opportunity to ascend to the island's pinnacle. This is reached by a 10km (6-mile) drive south of Santana, through the forest park of Pico das Pedras, up to **Achada do Teixeira** at 1,592 metres (5,223ft). From here, it is a two-hour round-trip walk to Pico Ruivo (see page 57).

The scenery northwest of Santana is just as delightful. **São Jorge** has a richly ornamented historic church, while past the village there is a splendid panorama from the *miradouro* at **Cabanas**, over to the valley of Arco de São Jorge.

The road winds inland towards the picturesque, fertile countryside around **Fajã do Penedo** and on to the pretty village of **Boaventura**. To cool off in a seafront lido, follow the coast road down to the small peninsula of **Ponta Delgada**, where the church next to the lido has a flamboyant ceiling painting depicting biblical stories. From here it's just 5km (3 miles) to São Vicente, at which point the road heads south to Ribeira Brava, then east back to Funchal.

EASTERN MADEIRA

The eastern section of Madeira is not as mountainous as the centre, but it has some wonderful coastal spots, a handful of attractive small towns, productive agricultural fields and a long, surreal promontory that juts out into the Atlantic.

Ponta de São Lourenço

As you head out of Funchal, the village of **Santo da Serra** ⑯ can be reached via Camacha or from the Poiso crossroads. The altitude of 670 metres (2,200ft) produces refreshing breezes, and explains why several wealthy British expats have chosen to build *quintas* here and why so many affluent Madeirans still flee the Funchal summer up into these hills.

The most striking feature of Santo da Serra is its flatness; it may not be in the league of Paúl da Serra, but it is still large enough to accommodate a 27-hole golf course (see page 87). Even if you're not much of a golfer, you might still enjoy a stroll through the pleasant gardens of **Quinta da Junta** (free), once owned by the ubiquitous Blandy family, but now open to the public. A lookout point provides views across to Machico on the coast, and you can enjoy a drink at the golf-club bar, set in what was once a *pousada*.

At **Portela** (662 metres/2,172ft), the views of the coast are striking. You may see hang-gliders taking off from a nearby platform. **Penha d'Águia** dominates the northeast coast. This huge rock formation, towering at 590 metres (1,935ft), levels off to a flat top. The name, meaning Eagle Rock, is derived from the eagles that once nested on ledges in its craggy cliff face.

The village of **Porto da Cruz**, 6km (4 miles) north, lies in the shadow of the rock. Here you will find one of Madeira's few sugar mills still working, pumping out steam as it processes the sugar cane to make *aguardente*, the local liquor, and molasses, which you can buy here.

MACHICO

Machico ⑰ is Madeira's first settlement, the spot where João Gonçalves Zarco first came ashore in 1419. Zarco ruled the southwestern half of Madeira, while his fellow Portuguese captain and navigator, Tristão Vaz Teixeira, governed the northeastern half from Machico. A statue of Teixeira stands outside the town's fifteenth-century parish church, **Igreja Matriz**. King Manuel I donated the statue of the Virgin (over the altar) and the distinguished church portal. The latter is a fine example of the exuberant style of Manueline architecture.

From Machico's triangular 'square', several streets lead to the beautifully landscaped seafront, home to a small custard-yellow fortress, built in 1706. Its battered walls contrast starkly with the ultramodern glass and concrete **Fórum Machico** cultural centre nearby. This exciting contemporary building has, besides two cinemas, a library and an auditorium, an inexpensive first-floor café and a ground-floor restaurant with panoramic views of Machico's wide bay. To the right, as you face the sea, is the tiny eighteenth-century **Capela de São Roque**, while the modern suspension bridge on the left of the bay leads to the **Capela dos Milagres** (Chapel of Miracles) built over the graves of Robert Machim and Anne d'Arfet, the first to set foot on Madeira (see page 17). Beyond the chapel, the town's former boatyard is now a picturesque marina, with shops and cafés. The 125-metre long Banda Além beach is distinguished for its yellow sand, imported from Morocco.

THE NORTHEAST COAST

The landscape of the extreme eastern peninsula, known as **Ponta de São Lourenço**, is more like Porto Santo (see page 66) and the Ilhas Desertas (see page 12) than Madeira. Keen walkers enjoy this wild, windswept tip of the island but, for all its wonderful views, it can be a bit too invigorating for comfort.

Close by, at **Prainha**, is the island's only natural sandy beach. Not surprisingly for a volcanic island, the sand here is black; the tiny beach can be crowded in high summer, but is deserted the rest of the year.

Nearby **Caniçal** ⑱ was once a whaling port, but since whaling was banned here in 1981, all that remains of this formerly lucrative industry is a museum and souvenirs on sale around the town. Although the **Museu da Baleia** (Whale Museum; www.museudabaleia.org; Tues–Sun 10am–6pm, last entry 4.30pm) shows a video of a local whale hunt from 1978, the owner is the epitome of a poacher-turned-gamekeeper. Once commander of the Caniçal whaling station and thus responsible for taking 100–200 of the great creatures each year, he now

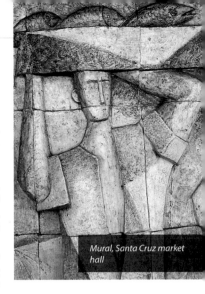

Mural, Santa Cruz market hall

devotes his energy to saving the whale and other marine life of the area. The 14-metre (45ft) model of the sperm whale is a reminder of the leviathans that once swam in great schools in the waters off Madeira. Whales are still sighted here, but not frequently. Caniçal remains a working fishing port, and has a selection of good fish restaurants.

Journeying back to Funchal from Caniçal via Machico, you will encounter the international airport, which serves the whole of Madeira. As you continue driving east, you actually travel underneath the runway, which is supported on huge pillars – a novel, if sobering, sensation.

Beyond the airport is the pleasant town of **Santa Cruz** ⑲, with an attractive church dating from the sixteenth century. Across the main square, the town hall retains a pair of splendid fifteenth- to sixteenth-century Manueline windows. A few streets away, the courthouse is another historic survivor, with fine verandas and an impressive main staircase. Along the seafront is the modern municipal market and a pebbly beach, while to the west of the town is the island's only waterpark, the **Aquaparque** (tel: 291 524 412; mid-May–mid-Sept daily 10am–6pm), with a series of slides, flumes, wave pools and other watery delights.

The main road along the coast towards Funchal passes **Caniço** ⓴, a village of two halves. Uphill is the original village, built around an imposing eighteenth-century church, with the pink-walled Quinta Splendida hotel just to the south offering the chance to explore its fine 'botanical' garden. Downhill, the Caniço de Baixo is a pretty garden suburb which is full of holiday villas and hotels set in lush vegetation, with a steep path down to a tiny beach which makes for a pleasant afternoon.

Roughly 2km (1 mile) further on, is **Ponta do Garajau**, a holiday development popular with German visitors. The road ends at a fine *miradouro*, where a statue of Christ stands with arms outstretched. There is also a splendid view west to the Bay of Funchal.

The road dropping down into Funchal winds past some of the town's smartest villas. The first landmark is the church of São Gonçalo in the parish of the same name; photographers love this spot for its classic views down to Funchal harbour. Also in the vicinity is a tiny, atmospheric chapel, which is dedicated to Nossa Senhora das Neves (Our Lady of the Snows).

PORTO SANTO

The island of Porto Santo, 40km (25 miles) northeast of Madeira, is the only other inhabited island in the archipelago, with a population of around 5,200. As desert islands go, it's not exactly undiscovered – it is accessible via a two-hour ferry crossing, or a very short (15min) flight – but only a handful of foreign visitors find these shores. Porto Santo is still, at heart, the resort of Madeirans, who seek what they have not: sand.

Porto Santo's prize is a 9km (6 mile) stretch of golden beach, but that's not all that distinguishes Porto Santo from Madeira. In summer the smaller island is scorched and yellow, with rust-coloured rock and cliff formations. The island is mostly quiet, apart from its three-month summer season. Out of season, even the main town seems deserted.

Porto Santo's idyllic beach

The frequently rough sea crossing drops passengers at Porto de Abrigo, on the eastern tip of the island. From the dock it is a short taxi or bus ride, or a 20-minute walk, to reach **Vila Baleira** ㉑ (sometimes referred to as **Porto Santo Town**), the island's only settlement of notable size.

VILA BALEIRA

The centre of Vila Baleira is a small, triangular plaza, comprising a little town hall and a restored church. **Nossa Senhora da Piedade** (Our Lady of Piety) was originally founded just after the island's discovery in the early to mid-fifteenth century. The present church was rebuilt after pirates destroyed the original in 1667, though part of it, the Morgada chapel, did survive.

Porto Santo's claim to fame, beyond its sandy beach, is its connection with Christopher Columbus. The town's major attraction is the rough-hewn **Casa Museu Cristóvão Colombo** (House-Museum of Christopher Columbus; tel: 291 983 405; Tues–Sat

10am–12.30pm & 2–5.30pm, Sun 10am–1pm), next to the church and dating from the fifteenth century.

The story of Columbus and the Madeiran archipelago is not entirely apocryphal, unlike so many other tales related to the islands. Columbus did marry Felipa Moniz Perestrelo, the granddaughter of the first governor of Porto Santo, Bartolomeu Perestrelo, but there is no strong evidence that this building was ever his home. That does not stop the museum claiming that Columbus lived here from 1478 to 1480 and that his tragically short-lived son, Diego, was born a *Portosantense* in this house.

Regardless of the truth, Casa Musei Cristóvão Colombo is worth a visit. Displays include period pieces, memorabilia, replicas, maps, paintings and sketches, but no personal effects or anything directly linked to the man himself. Another curious enigma about Columbus that has baffled historians is that no reliable likeness of him has ever survived. Look at the many different and imaginary portraits in the museum and then compare them with the dashing, modern bust of him in the public gardens by the quay.

The liveliest street in Vila Baleira is Rua João Gonçalves Zarco, situated on the other side of the river from the plaza, and lined by a handicraft centre, shopping mall and several charming old shops and bars. The main square is Largo do Pelourinho (Pillory Square), where, as the name indicates, local offenders were once punished.

AN ISLAND TOUR

Porto Santo is tiny – less than 11km (6 miles) by 6km (4 miles). It does not require much sightseeing, which is good, because most people just come to bake on the beach. Hiring a car is expensive, and what there is to see is usually near the main roads.

Taxis will take you around the island, giving their own tours at fixed prices (see page 128). Pick up a leaflet from the tourist office and ask for a driver who can speak your language.

Heading counter-clockwise around the island, the first stop is the lookout point of **Portela** (163 metres/535ft). From here, you can survey the 9km (5.6 miles) swathe of golden sand. Head north, however, and the desolate nature of the landscape is inescapable. Crop yields are poor, partly because of the chronic lack of water, and land that was once tended is now deserted. For most people, earning a living from tourism is more appealing than toiling in the fields.

The island's highest peak, at 517 metres (1,695ft), is **Pico do Facho** ㉒, around 1.5km (1 mile) north of Portela. You will need hiking boots to get to the summit. Its name, which means Peak of the Torch, derives from the warning beacons that were lit here in the days when French and Algerian pirates posed a threat to the island.

The circular road now arcs north to the diminutive village of **Camacha**, where the Museu Cardina (Wed 10.30am–6.30pm,

Portela's windmills

Thurs–Sat 10.30am–12.30pm & 2.30–6.30pm) centres on a picturesque old windmill and has models and tools illustrating the area's past. Nearby, a ramshackle winery with an antique wooden press produces the local Porto Santo wine. If it is closed, you can still sample the wine in one of the village's collection of bars.

A minor road heads west out of Camacha to **Fonte da Areia** (Sand Spring), where the rugged coastline is particularly lovely. Sandstone cliffs and rocks have been weathered into interesting shapes and small caves. A spring filtering through the rocks is the source of the island's mineral water, said to guarantee eternal youth.

The main road continues its loop, almost bringing you back to Vila Baleira, before a minor road heads north again towards **Pico do Castelo**. It is only a couple of hundred metres from Pico do Facho, and from its height of 437 metres (1,433ft), accessible by car, it provides a commanding view itself.

The old, rusted cannons are all that remain of the fortifications that once protected the islanders from pirates – it is a popular spot

FALSE PROPHETS, MAGICAL SANDS

The inhabitants of Porto Santo are sometimes referred to by Madeirans as *profetas* (prophets) – the result of a strange episode in the sixteenth century, when a local shepherd started a religious cult. Not only did he claim to be able to predict the future, he held people in sway by saying he had the power to list their most intimate secrets and sins. Fortunately, the cult was short-lived, and the *Portosantenses* resumed normality.

Magical powers of a different kind are attributed to the island's beach, which is said to hold curative properties that alleviate all kinds of aches and pains. Many Madeirans are convinced of its benefits and bury themselves up to their necks in sand.

Exploring Calhau da Serra on a quad bike

for picnics and barbecues. Porto Santo's Airport lies just below; beyond it is the vivid green of Porto Santo's golf course, contrasting with the tawny hues of the rest of the island.

A favourite picnic spot is **Morenos**, which is located towards the southwest tip of the island, although it is close to, and looking out over, the north coast. It is neat and well-tended with plenty of sunshades, flowers and seats, and enjoys a picturesque view over to the little **Ilhéu de Ferro** (Isle of Iron). The last viewpoint of the tour to be found is **Pico das Flores**, at 184 metres (603ft).

Directly beneath Pico das Flores is the southern end of the beach and Porto Santo's southwest tip, which is known as **Ponta da Calheta**. The rest of the island's beach is an uninterrupted expanse, backed by attractive but slightly featureless dunes. Here, however, there are small bays with rocky outcrops to be found and you can also enjoy a beautiful view which stretches across to the Ilhéu de Baixo. It makes a fantastic afternoon of exploring.

Carnaval celebrations in Funchal

THINGS TO DO

SHOPPING

Madeira is an outstanding shopping destination, given its long craft heritage. The island is renowned for wicker items, exquisite handmade lace and embroidery, gorgeous flowers and local wines. Traditional, labour-intensive methods and quality are still respected in Madeira. Unlike the Canary Islands, Madeira offers no tax concessions for visiting shoppers, so this is not the place to come in search of cheap electrical items, designer clothes, cameras or watches.

BEST BUYS

Wicker

You will find an outstanding array of wicker items: linen, shopping and picnic baskets, tables, chairs and trays. While many items are attractive and inexpensive, the impracticality of taking them home might suggest opting for more convenient souvenirs. Accustomed to exporting, though, most companies will gladly send large items to Europe and North America for you.

The wicker industry started in the 1850s in Camacha, and this parish is still the wicker capital of Madeira. Wickerwork in the making is far more interesting than it sounds: items are crafted with hands and feet, and occasionally teeth as well.

Needlework

Madeira's hand embroidery is unsurpassed. This

Midday breaks

Madeirans do not take a midday siesta, but most businesses, including shops, close for a one- or two-hour lunch break.

Handmade embroidery

disappearing art form – still going strong in Madeira – is an amalgam of styles and techniques that has evolved over more than 150 years. Along with fortified wine, embroidery and lacemaking are Madeira's superlative exports, and in Funchal you have ample opportunity to visit factories or workshops where the final touches are put to these painstakingly produced items. Madeira creates and exports table linens, sheets, dresses, blouses, handkerchiefs and even wedding dresses of extraordinary delicacy.

If you are used to machine-made, mass-produced embroidered items, you may be in for a price-tag shock – a full set of meticulously detailed table linens can take up to two years to make, so they aren't cheap.

To be sure that any needlework item is genuine, look for a lead seal (or a hologram) with an 'M', the emblem of IVBAM. This seal confirms the piece has been certified by the Instituto do Vinho, do Bordado, Artesanato e Bebidas Espirituosas da Madeira (Institute of Wine, Embroidery and Handicrafts of Madeira; https://ivbam.madeira.gov.pt), an official island organisation that has a museum on Rua Visconde de Anadia 44 (Mon–Fri 9am–12.30pm, 2–5.30pm). There you will find a tapestry known as the *Allegory of Madeira*, which employed 14 young women over a period of three years and contains an estimated 7-million stitches.

Other handicrafts

Though wicker and needlework are the biggest sellers, other craft items also make good souvenirs and gifts. **Boots** made from soft goatskin are part of the national costume. The boot and leather goods seller just outside the entrance of Funchal's Mercado dos Lavradores is worth a visit. The boots worn by the *carreiros*, the sled-men who push the Monte toboggans, are also available (as are the **straw** boaters, that they wear).

Ceramics and pottery are some of the most popular items on sale throughout Portugal. However, most of the items you will find in Madeira, such as pretty hand-painted plates, planters, jugs and jars, come from the mainland.

Other items include **marquetry**, a revived island craft that is featured on small boxes, pictures and furniture. The **brinquinho**

Traditional knitwear for sale

Bring a bird of paradise home

is Madeira's answer to the tambourine, in which miniature cymbals are clashed together by costumed dolls 'dancing' round a maypole. You will find thick **knitwear** – pullovers, hats and gloves and plenty more – at many shops up in the mountains. Many of these wintry items are imported from the north of **Portugal** and make great souvenirs.

Food and drink

Madeira cake and wine are extremely long-lasting, so you can safely bring some back home. Genuine Madeira cake, *bolo de mel* (honey cake), sold in many different sizes, is very different from what you get at home; it is a delicious, dark, heavy cake, similar to gingerbread. Despite its name, it is made from molasses, not honey. It lasts for up to a year and goes very well with a dry Madeira wine. You will also find plentiful supplies of traditional biscuits, honey, jams and marmalades.

Most visitors take home a bottle or two of Madeira wine (see page 99). Connoisseurs with money to burn hunt down vintage bottles – you can still turn up rare bottles like a 1795 Barbeito Terrantez or 1900 Malvasia Solera (Henriques & Henriques).

Other alcoholic drinks that you might want to take home include *branquinha* (*aguardente* with a stick of sugar cane in the bottle), or a local liqueur such as *licor de maracujá* (passionfruit) or *ginja* (cherry liqueur).

Collectables

Madeira is not noted for antiques, but stamps, coins, banknotes and vintage postcards are of interest to many collectors. A shop specialising in these items is at Avenida Arriaga 75 (Marina Shopping Centre, Shop C; tel: 291 223 070).

Flowers

Recreating a lush Madeiran garden isn't easy, but you can still take home souvenir flamingo flowers (*anthuriums*), orchids and bird of paradise flowers (*strelitzias*, or *estelícias* in Portuguese). The latter in particular will last quite a while after your return home. Most shops will box these for storage in the aircraft hold and deliver them either to your hotel or the airport on the day you leave. Orchid plants and flowers can be purchased all over the island at flower stands, markets and in florist shops.

Where to shop

Funchal's central area contains the best variety of shops and local products on the island. The main shopping streets are Fernão Ornelas, Ferreiros, Queimada de Cima and Queimada de Baixo. The city has transformed in recent years, large shopping centres stock the major brands and ubiquitous high-street chains have sprung up alongside classic boutiques.

For the best possible introduction to all of the island's handicrafts and saleable products, visit the **Casa do Turista** (Rua do Conselheiro and José Silvestre Ribeiro 2; tel: 291 236 343) on the seafront. The first few rooms are carefully laid out with pieces of antique shelving displaying fragile breakable items; beyond them, you will find a fairly conventional department store that stocks Portuguese ceramics, porcelain, wines, embroidery, dolls and inexpensive souvenirs. Out the back on the terrace is a 'mini-village', where a little *palheiro* (see page 60), a house with a weaving

Brightly costumed flower seller in Funchal's market

loom and an old-fashioned shop, re-creates a bit of old Madeira.

For needlework, visit any of Funchal's factories, which put the finishing touches on items and act principally as showrooms, selling direct to the public. The biggest is **Patrício & Gouveia Sucessores** (Rua do Visconde de Anadia 34; tel: 291 220 801; www. patriciogouveia.pt); it offers weekday tours. Keep an eye out for other outlets marked by small signs in doorways, including **Bazar Oliveiras** (Rua das Murcas 6; tel: 291 224 632) and **Madeira Supérbia** (Rua do Carmo 27; tel: 291 226 650).

Wicker products are offered everywhere in Funchal – you will find one of the biggest shops in Rua do Castanheiro – and all over Madeira, but the main centre for wickerwork with the biggest choice is located in the village of Camacha. It is Madeira's 'All Things Wicker', with items ranging from the most conventional to the most implausible.

There are flower sellers along Avenida Arriaga near the Sé (Cathedral) as well as inside the **Mercado dos Lavradores** (Mon–Fri 7am–6pm, Sun 8am–2pm). A shop specialising in selling and packaging flowers for long-distance transport is **Loja de Flores - A Flor da Ajuda** (Rua Velha de Ajuda; tel: 291 763 242).

For Madeira wines, the most atmospheric place to shop is the **Adegas de São Francisco** (see page 29; www.

blandyswinelodge.com) in Avenida Arriaga next to the tourist office. It has tasting rooms where you can even try vintage wines dating from 1920, a shop selling the four brands now owned by the Madeira Wine Company (Blandy's, Cossart Gordon, Miles and Leacock), a book and souvenir shop, and a pleasant café. Other possibilities for purchasing wine in Funchal include the **Pérola dos Vinhos** (Rua da Alfândega; www.peroladosvinhos.com) and various brands are available in supermarkets. The winery and shop of **Henriques & Henriques Vinhos**, producers of award-winning wines, is located in Câmara de Lobos (Avenida Nova Cidade; tel: 291 941 551; www.henriqueschenriques.pt).

If you have run out of things to read by the pool, make sure to check out **Bertrand Bookstore** (CC La Vie Funchal, Rua Dr Brito Câmara 19; tel: 291 280 022) or the old-fashioned **Livraria Esperança** (Rua dos Ferreiros 156; tel: 291 221 116). Here you will discover thousands of used books, and some of them are in English.

COLOURFUL CHARACTERS

Madeiran street flower sellers wear traditional costume – not only good for business, but required by law. Ladies in cheerful garb, as colourful as the flowers they hawk, gather alongside the cathedral at the main city market.

Younger girls wear the same red and yellow striped skirts, often with a red bolero jacket and red cape, for folk-dance demonstrations. Men wear white linen trousers and white shirts, with red cummerbunds. Black skullcaps, with curly tassels like candle wicks, are worn by both men and women, as are the native *botachã* (literally, plain boots), made from tanned ox hide and goat skin. Women's boots are distinguished by a red band (see page 75).

ENTERTAINMENT

Madeira does not rank with the Balearic or Canary Islands in terms of lively, nighttime entertainment; it's much more of a low-key place than that. Although Funchal has a few pubs, bars, discos and even a well-attended casino with revues, the majority of visitors do not come to the island in search of a hedonistic nightlife.

The nucleus of the tourist-nightlife scene consists mainly of the major hotels and their bars and nightclubs. At Funchal's **Casino da Madeira** (Avenida do Infante; tel: 291 140 424; www.casino-damadeira.com; Sun–Thurs 3pm–3am, Fri & Sat 4pm–4am), in the grounds of the Pestana Casino Park hotel, you can play blackjack and roulette, and take a turn at the slot machines. An admission fee is charged, which covers a free drink and some gambling chips. You will need to take your passport if you wish to do more than hit the ground-level slot machines; the real gambling is upstairs.

NIGHTLIFE

If gambling isn't your scene, the casino entertainment complex goes for the *tropicália* quotient with its **Copacabana Nightclub** (tel: 291 140 424; Fri, Sat & bank hols 11pm–3am; select dates until 4am), with live bands and DJs sets. The other principal hotel for nightlife is the Pestana Carlton Madeira (see page 135), which puts on themed evenings, plus classical concerts and children's shows.

Young people head for the **Café do Teatro** (Avenida Arriaga, next to the municipal theatre; tel: 291 226 371), **Madeira Rum House** (Rua Portão de São Tiago 19; www.madeirarumhouse.com; tel: 966 017 555) and the wine bar O Americano right in the heart of Funchal (Rua da Carreira 120; tel: 967 925 452). **Trap Music Bar** (Rua do Favilla 7; tel: 915 006 659) close to Hotel Pestana Carlton is a trendy place spread over three levels with nightly live music and

Fireworks over Funchal's harbour during the Atlantic Festival

a lovely rooftop bar. For excellent, wallet-friendly drinks head to **Hole in One** at Estrada Monumental 238A (tel: 291 765 443) which has a lovely garden under banana trees. Cocktail bar 23 Vintage (Rua Santa Maria 23; tel: 914 758 975) has good vibes and DJs bringing back the spirit of the 1970s, 1980s and 1990s.

For more down-to-earth nightlife, two places offer regular *fado* evenings. These are **Arsénio's** restaurant (Rua de Santa Maria 169; tel: 966 300 834; fado Tues, Thurs & Fri 8–10pm) and **Sabor a Fado** (Travessa das Torres 10; tel: 925 612 259; 6pm–1am), where even the waitresses can sing fado. Wailing *fado* songs, accompanied by classical guitar, generally deal with the hardships of love and life. Folk-dancing evenings are a regular feature at hotels and local tour companies will arrange folklore evenings at a restaurant where some of Madeira's very best folk dancers give a performance.

Funchal's **Teatro Municipal** (http://teatro.cm-funchal.pt) is the only place that regularly stages theatrical entertainment. It is

Folk dancers in Funchal

worth a visit, if only to see the theatre itself. Dating from 1888, it has been restored to its original splendour, and produces most of the performing arts. It is the centrepiece of the annual **Atlantic Festival** held in June. This festival attracts some of the big names in the classical music world, and the best of the concerts are broadcast on the island's radio station.

Throughout the year, students and teachers from the Madeira Music Conservatoire perform at atmospheric venues such as the Quinta das Cruzes museum (see page 34). Visit the tourist office on Avenida Arriaga for further concert information.

FESTIVALS

Madeira's major festivals are: Carnival, Flower Festival, Wine Festival and New Year's Eve. As long as you don't mind the crowds, these can be the best time to visit the island.

CARNIVAL

Staged in February (occasionally in March), the pre-Lenten **Carnaval** (Carnival) is celebrated in the streets of Funchal with Brazilian-style samba rhythms. However, don't expect the hedonism or sensuality of the celebrations in Rio, Salvador or Tenerife – Funchal is too restrained for that.

FLOWER FESTIVAL

The **Festa da Flor**, held in late April or early May, is a crowd-pleaser. Floats – decorated in beautiful, inventive floral creations – parade through Funchal's streets. Two events peripheral to the main parade should not be missed. One is the **children's parade**,

DANCE ROOTS

Many of Madeira's music and dance traditions date back to the island's colonisation. They evoke rural and courtship rituals, as well as less happy moments in the island's history. Dances reflect the importance of labour: jaunty jigs mimic the crushing of grapes with bare feet (a practice much rarer now than it once was) and slower numbers act out the carrying of heavy baskets.

The 'Dance of the Ponta do Sol' – which harks back to Ponta do Sol's days as slave quarters – is a somber affair. The steps are short; the feet, as if chained, hardly lift off the ground; and the head is submissively bowed (enslaved people were forbidden to look their masters in the eye).

Two of the musical instruments played are uniquely Madeiran: the *machête*, a guitar-like instrument plucked to a rather monotonous beat; and the extraordinary *brinquinho*, a percussion instrument that features tiny folk-dancing dolls holding bells and castanets.

Funchal's Flower Festival

in which each child carries a single flower and places it in a hole in a 'Wall of Hope' in the Praça do Município. Once the parade is finished, an **exhibition** of the award-winning displays is staged in a lovely old house in Rua dos Castanheiros.

WINE FESTIVAL

Festivals commence at the end of August in wine villages, such as Estreito de Câmara de Lobos, to celebrate the September harvest. You may occasionally see grapes being crushed the traditional way: barefoot men and women treading the grapes. Wine samples are also served from traditional goatskin bags once used to store and carry wine.

NEW YEAR'S EVE

Madeira's biggest and most spectacular festival has an international reputation. Every year, Funchal's hotels are packed, and you will need to book accommodation many months in advance and pay a hefty premium. Several winter cruise ships anchor in Funchal harbour on 31 December to participate in the party. At midnight, all the houses in town switch on all their lights, opening all the doors and windows, setting the hillside ablaze with light. The cruise ships crank up their floodlights, and the parties begin. As the New Year rings in, a splendid and exciting fireworks display erupts.

RELIGIOUS FESTIVALS

Several **religious festivals** also take place throughout the year, but one especially stands out – the **Feast of the Assumption**, which is known more parochially as the Festival of Nossa Senhora do Monte (Our Lady of Monte), is celebrated on 15 August in Monte. Pilgrims flock from all around the island to kiss the image of the patron saint, and some ascend the final 68 steps to the church on their knees.

To the many Madeirans who believe that the Lady of Monte has carried them through troubled times, the pilgrimage is an obligation. For these people the Monte church is akin to Lourdes. The sick and infirm arrive in droves in search of miraculous cures. Once the pious devotions are over, wine flows, fireworks explode and *espetada* (kebab) stalls flourish, before Monte regains normality for another 364 days.

SPORTS

With no beaches to speak of, and scarcely enough flat ground for a playing surface, Madeira may not be the first destination that springs to mind for a sporting holiday. However, there are sufficient opportunities for most active holiday-makers and excellent ones for those who enjoy walking, hiking and climbing.

SPECTATOR SPORTS

The only sport to watch on Madeira is **football**. Islanders are wild about *futebol*, and two of the island's teams – Marítimo (www.csmaritimo.org.pt) and Nacional (www.csmaritimo.org.pt). Marítimo play in the Primeira Liga of the Portuguese league and their stadium is on Rua Dr Pita. Nacional were relegated to Liga 2 in 2021 and their stadium is high above Funchal at Choupana. The latter discovered the talent of Cristiano Ronaldo, who played for Nacional until he was 12.

WALKING & HIKING

Mountainous Madeira, with its network of *levada* trails (see page 60), is perfect for walkers of all ages and abilities. Such watercourses exist elsewhere, but nowhere are they so accessible nor do they cover such a great area. The island's irrigation system is composed of some 2,100km (1,300 miles) of channels. The paths that run alongside them are mostly gentle but exhilarating at the same time. More serious trekkers, with cross-country or mountain walking on their minds, can choose from one of the walks listed below:

Boca da Corrida–Encumeada (moderate; 6hr): views of Curral das Freiras and Ribeiro do Poco valley. **Pico do Arieiro–Pico Ruivo–Achada do Teixeira** (moderate–difficult; 4hr): a trip to Madeira's

The footpaths alongside levadas make great walking trails

highest peak. **Ponta de São Lourenço** (moderate; 4hr): great rock formations, flora and views of the Atlantic. **The Caniçal tunnel–Boca do Risca–Larano** (moderate; 5hr): a walk along the north coast between Boca do Risco and Porto da Cruz; terrific flora and sea views.

All these can be undertaken alone by experienced walkers or with local guides (see page 119), but it is best to know in advance what you are likely to encounter and a reliable walkers' guidebook (see page 124) is a good investment.

> **Advice for hikers**
>
> If you are going to do some of Madeira's serious walking trails, take warm clothing, as the weather can change very abruptly. Hiking boots with good support and traction are a sensible idea to combat uneven or loose surfaces, and sunblock is essential.

GOLF

This is a year-round sport in Madeira. The island has 45 holes of championship golf divided between two courses, both of which are esteemed for their scenic beauty. Having staged the Madeira Island Open on 20 occasions (part of the PGA European Tour), the 27-hole **Clube de Golf Santo da Serra** (tel: 291 550 100; www.santodaserragolf.com) is one of Europe's most exciting courses, suitable for all levels. Designed by Robert Trent Jones, the course is close to the picturesque village of Santo da Serra, east of Funchal, and has stupendous views to the sea below. The **Palheiro Golf Club** (tel: 291 790 120; www.palheirogolf.com) is in the São Gonçalo hills, 15 minutes east of the centre of Funchal. The course, designed by Cabell Robinson, has 18 holes and is set in the Quinta do Palheiro Ferreiro gardens. So spectacular are the views over the bay and city that it is a great place to visit, even if you don't play golf. On Porto Santo, the **Porto Santo Golfe** (tel:

291 983 778; www.portosantogolfe.com) is an 18-hole course designed by Seve Ballesteros and located in a green valley on the slopes of the Pico Ana Ferreira mountain, with sea breezes and coastal scenery.

TENNIS

Flat land is at such a premium in Funchal that even the likes of Reid's Palace and the Royal Savoy can only afford two tennis courts each. If your hotel does not have its own court, try **Funchal Tennis Club** (tel: 291 763 237) which offers private and group lessons.

TRAIL RUNNING

The island's *levadas* and mountain paths are a paradise for trail runners, who can participate in several competitions throughout

A lido complex in Porto da Cruz

the year, including the prestigious Madeira Island Ultra Trail (MIUT; www.madeiraultratrail.com). The most challenging MIUT category is a hefty 115km (70-mile) course with steep climbs, varied terrain and unpredictable weather conditions – not for the faint of heart.

HORSE RIDING

Lessons and cross-country riding are offered by the **Associação Hípica da Madeira** (Quinta Villa Alpires, Caminho dos Pretos, São João Latrão; tel: 966 720 153), just outside Funchal. Horse riding can also be arranged at **Quinta do Riacho** (tel: 967 010 015; www.quintadoriacho.com), and the **CEM** (tel: 291 552 135; www.clubeequestremadeira.com), and on the island of Porto Santo at the **Centro Hípico** (tel: 291 983 258).

SWIMMING

Although much of Madeira's coast drops dizzily into the sea, offering little or no safe access for bathers, there is an artificial beach with imported golden sand at Calheta (and Machico), and a number of **lido complexes** around the coast offering swimming pools and cafés, along with concrete jetties that lead out to safe sea bathing and diving areas. Among the best are the lidos at Seixal, Ponta Delgada, Ponta Gorda and Porto da Cruz. For something more natural, there is the small black-sand beach at Prainha and the bathing complex east of São Jorge. You can also have a dip in the semi-natural pools at **Porto Moniz** on the island's extreme northwest tip, or enjoy slides and flumes at Santa Cruz's **Aquaparque** (see page 66).

Beach lovers should hop islands to the 9km (6 miles) of sand at **Porto Santo** (though sunshine is only really guaranteed between June and August). You can fly with TAP Air Portugal (15min flight) or take the daily ferry at 8am (tel: 291 210 300; www.portosanto-line.pt).

Diving is popular on Madeira

Most of the good hotels have swimming pools and there is a year-round swimming pool open to the public at the **Complexo Balnear do Lido** (Lido Complex; tel: 291 105 760; www.frentemar-funchal.com) in Funchal's Tourist Zone. There are two main pools, plus a children's pool, sunbathing along the terraces and rocks by the sea, and good catering facilities. What's more, it's cheap. Other options include **Complexo Balnear da Barreirinha**, right next to the **São Tiago Fortress**, as well as the excellent **Funchal Olympic Swimming Pool Complex** (Mon–Fri 8am–6pm, Sat 8am–noon; tel: 291 741 173), which consists of four pools including an Olympic one.

DIVING

Divers are in luck in Madeira, since one of Europe's first under-water nature reserves was created along the Garajau coastline. Besides abundant, colourful fish, divers can see shipwrecks. Sea temperatures vary between 18° and 24°C (64 and 75°F). Several diving schools are recommended. **Manta Diving Centre** (tel: 291 935 588; www.mantadiving.com), based in Caniço east along the coast from Funchal, offers wreck-, night-, cave- and Nitrox-diving. **Focus Natura** based in Santa Cruz at Ribeira de Boaventura (tel: 916 409 780; www.focusnatura.com), offers everything from beginners' courses and single dives to advanced tuition. Alternatively, the **Madeira Dive Point** at the Pestana Carlton Madeira Hotel (tel: 291 239 579; www.madeiradivepoint.com), offers diving equipment for hire, and various courses. A single dive costs around €35, while a novice-diving course, including equipment hire, will run to €350 or more.

BIG GAME FISHING AND BOAT TRIPS

In the deep Atlantic, just beyond Madeira's shallow waters, you can catch – depending on the season – giant blue marlin, bonito, tuna (big-eye, blue-fin and yellow-fin), barracuda, swordfish, wahoo and shark (hammerhead, mako and blue). Madeira's sport-fishing companies operate a 'tag and release' scheme whereby any fish caught are returned unharmed to the wild after photographing.

The very best deep-sea fishing is from June to September. **Madeira Sight Casting** (tel: 917 846 244; www.madeirasight-casting.com) charters set out from Funchal Marina. Captain Peter Bristow of **Fish Madeira** (Travessa das Virtudes, Sao Martinho 23, 9000–163 Funchal; tel: 917 599 990; www.fishmadeira.com) also runs big-game fishing expeditions. Big-game fishing expeditions generally cost upwards of €200 per person per day.

CHILDREN'S MADEIRA

Madeira has several attractions aimed at families, including the **Madeira Story Centre** in Funchal (see page 36), with

Children will enjoy a cable-car ride

computers and interactive games based on Madeira's history. The **Madeira Theme Park** in Santana (see page 60) has adventure playgrounds and a boating lake; the **Aquarium** (tel: 291 850 340) in Porto Moniz and the São Vicente **Caves and Volcanism Centre** (see page 53) are also likely to appeal. Given all these choices, most children should find a visit to the island an enjoyable experience, especially if it coincides with any of the major festivals (see page 82 and Calendar of Events, page 93). The festivals with greatest appeal for children are the famous **Flower Festival**, with the children's parade and 'Wall of Hope', and the exciting **Carnaval**. When all else fails, the swimming pools (see page 89) are enough to satisfy almost any child or teenager and makes for plenty of family holiday fun in Madeira.

If you don't want to hire a car, both the **Jardim Botânico** (see page 39), with its bird park, and the **Palheiro Gardens** (see page 40) are accessible by bus. The park on the hill of **Monte** makes an excellent playground.

Activities for slightly older children include horse riding and *levada* walks. A very enjoyable nature day – identifying plants and flowers, dipping toes into the refreshing irrigation canals, cooling off in tunnels, picnicking on a hillside – can be had at any of the *levada* paths highlighted in this book.

WHAT'S ON

5 January *Festa dos Reis/Cantar os Reis* (Singing of the Kings): Funchal and elsewhere. Santo Amaro Festival and close of Christmas festivities.

Late January *São Sebastião* celebrated in Caniçal, Câmara de Lobos.

February/March The biennial Festival of Wine, Embroidery & Handicrafts of Madeira.

Carnaval: huge festival in Funchal, culminating in a colourful procession on the Saturday before Shrove Tuesday (see page 83).

May *Festa da Flor* (Flower Festival): floral floats parade through Funchal, also the Children's Parade and Wall of Hope (see page 83).

June Atlantic Festival: weekend musical performances in Funchal's Teatro Municipal and other venues, and firework displays over the harbour.

23–24 June *São João da Ribeira* (Feast of St John) celebrated in Funchal, São João, Câmara de Lobos, Ponta do Sol and elsewhere.

29 June *São Pedro* (St Peter), patron saint of fishermen: bonfires and boat procession at Ribeira Brava, Ponta do Pargo and Câmara de Lobos.

1 July *Dia da Madeira* (Madeira Day): Madeirans celebrate political autonomy from Portugal. Events across Madeira.

Mid-July *Festa da Cereja* (Cherry Festival) in Jardim da Serra, Câmara de Lobos: a weekend of sport and culture to celebrate the cherry harvest. Funchal Jazz Festival: top national and international musicians perform.

Late July *24 Horas a Bailar*: 24-hour folk-dance marathon, Santana.

14–15 August *Festa da Nossa Senhora do Monte* (Our Lady of Monte): pilgrims flock to Monte from all around the island.

25 August–11 September Madeira Wine Festival: grape harvesting in Estreito de Câmara de Lobos, with shows and exhibitions here and in Funchal.

Mid-September Columbus Festival in Porto Santo: music concerts and street parades celebrate the great navigator.

October Madeira Nature Festival: adventure and cultural activities for all ages. Madeira Organ Festival: 10-day musical feast.

1 November *Festa da Castanha* (Chestnut Festival) in Curral das Freiras. Funchal International Film Festival: a week-long event.

December Christmas illuminations and fireworks on New Year's Eve.

FOOD AND DRINK

Funchal has been catering for visitors since Victorian times. While it's not Portugal's dining capital, there are plenty of good restaurants. For international or haute cuisine, the best places are in the hotel zone, the up-market, far end of the Old Town, and the touristy marina establishments. If you would rather eat with local people, try the side streets around the cathedral, Rua Carreira or cafés along Rua Dom Carlos I.

Most Madeiran restaurants stick to traditional opening times, with lunch *(almoço)* served from around noon to 3pm and dinner *(jantar)* from 7 to 10pm. Many restaurants in Funchal offer all-day service, not closing after lunch, and you will never have any problems finding cafés serving snacks all day. For breakfast *(pequeno almoço)*, most Madeirans start their day with a sweet pastry and coffee. Hotels usually serve the standard international buffet, with bacon and egg, cold meats, cheeses, fruit and cereals.

WHAT TO EAT

Madeira has its own typical dishes, in addition to Portuguese specialities. As a rule, the food here is simple; it uses fresh ingredients and is served up in hearty portions. A Madeiran trademark is the excellent island bread, *bolo do caco*, which is made from flour and sweet potato and normally served with garlic butter *(manteiga de alho)*.

Seasoning savvy

Salt and pepper are not usually placed on the table. But you will be given them if you ask: *sal e pimenta, faz favor.*

Starters. Soup is always on the menu. The best is usually Madeira's *own tomate e cebola*, a delicious soup made from tomatoes and onions,

The breathtaking view from the terrace at Villa Cipriani

and very often served *com ovo* (with a poached egg floating on top). A Portuguese staple, *caldo verde* (literally green broth), is a thick soup of potato puree with finely shredded cabbage or kale. Another soup from the mainland is *açorda*, thicker still and made with bread and garlic.

Basic fish restaurants serve *caramujos* (winkles), which look unappetising as you prise them out from their tiny shells, but taste fine, and *lupus grelhadas* (grilled limpets). The latter are a meatier version of mussels (some of them taste almost like liver) and are served grilled in the shell. At the other end of the price spectrum, look out for smoked swordfish *(espadarte fumado)*, a Portuguese delicacy that is a little like smoked salmon, but tastes less sweet and has a coarser texture.

Fish and seafood. Madeira's speciality, seen on menus across the island, is the *espada*, a fearsome-looking, ink-black, eel-like beast, which can grow to around 1 metre (3ft) in length and has long, needle-sharp teeth. Despite its appearance, this nasty creature has delicious white meat. Some restaurants serve it poached, but more often fillets are fried, often with a banana, which complements the flavour surprisingly well. Note that *espada* and *espadarte* (sword-fish; see page 95), though similar-sounding, are different fish.

The other island fish is tuna (*atum*), often served in steaks (*bife de atum*) and with a Madeira-wine sauce (*a Madeirense*). Maize or cornmeal (*milho*) deep-fried in cubes (also an island speciality) is often served with tuna, and is offered as a standard accompaniment to many meals in rustic restaurants around the island.

You will find a wide selection of other fish on the menu, usually grilled or fried, including: *pargo* and *besugo*, which are types of sea bream; *garoupa* and *cherne*, types of grouper; and *bacalhau*, the famous salt-cod, cooked in many different ways. It is often served

Grilled limpets are a speciality; they taste better than they look

in a casserole, which tends to hide its distinctive, preserved flavour. Try it *cozido* (boiled). Other fish are shark, sword-fish and *bodião* (parrot-fish).

Two slow-simmering Portuguese favourites that appear on restaurant menus are *caldeirada*, a rich stew made from fish, potato, tomato and onion, and *cata-plana*. The latter is named after the hinged pressure cooker made of copper that is used to cook a mixture of clams, ham, sausage, onion, garlic, parsley, white wine and paprika (ingre-dients vary from one restaurant to the next).

> **Free food?**
>
> Most restaurants serve an assortment of appetisers, including bread and butter, which appears to be free but usually isn't. You will be charged anything from €1 to €5 for the items. If you do not touch them, however, you should not, in theory, be charged for them.

Two local favourites are octopus (*polvo*), served cold in a salad or hot, fried or stewed; and squid (*lulas*), grilled, fried or stuffed (*rec-heado*). Shellfish do not flourish in Madeiran waters, and all prawns and lobsters are imported.

A menu that quotes a price – usually for shellfish or fresh fish – as *'preço V'* means variable, or market, price. Ascertain the day's market price before ordering.

Meat. *Espetada* (not to be confused with *espada* or *espadarte*) is the typical Madeiran meat dish, a kebab of beef traditionally threaded on a skewer of sweet bay. In many restaurants, however, it is served on a metal skewer with a hook on one end, which is hung vertically from a special stand fixed to the end of your dining table. The beef is first grilled over embers of fragrant sweet bay, having been marinated in garlic and wine to make it tender and tasty – though it can occasionally still be tough. For something easier on the jaw, try pork in wine and garlic (*porco de vinho e alho*), which is marinated, tenderised and then grilled. Chicken (*frango*) is always on the menu, and may be served plain, grilled, African-style (as in *piri-piri*, when it's basted in a sauce of hot chilli peppers, then grilled) or in a Goan-inspired curry sauce. Ox tongue (*língua*) served with Madeira-wine sauce is also a Portuguese speciality.

Desserts. *Pudim de leite* (milk pudding) is common, as is *gelado* (ice cream). A good restaurant will offer seasonal fruit after your meal, but you may have to ask for it. The island has an excellent range of exotic fruits, so sample them fresh from the market if not in a restaurant. A favourite is *anonas* or custard apple (originally from Peru). Split in half, the flesh is soft and white, with large black pips. Other popular desserts include *malassadas* (a deep-fried yeast dough served with sugar cane honey) and *bolo de mel* (honey cake).

The fearsome-looking espadas

TABLE WINES

There are various varieties of Madeiran table wine, of which Atlantis Rosé is the most famous, sold across the island. Most good restaurants stock a full complement of Portuguese wines (top restaurants will also offer foreign labels), many of which are excellent.

You need do nothing more than tell the waiter *tinto* (red) or *branco* (white), and you can't go wrong. However, several of the best wine-producing regions have names whose use is controlled by law (denominação de origem controlada), and it's worth seeking out wines from the best regions. Dão and Douro in the north of Portugal produce vigorous reds and flavourful whites. Wines from the Alentejo region are also highly regarded.

Vinho Verde (literally green wine), popular all over Portugal, is named for its youth, rather than its colour, and has a slight fizz. It goes well with simple fish and seafood dishes.

The two most celebrated Portuguese wines, port and Madeira, are primarily known as dessert wines, but they may also be sipped as aperitifs. The before-dinner varieties are dry or extra dry white port, and dry or medium-dry Madeira wines (Sercial, Terrantez and Verdelho). These should be served slightly chilled. After dinner, sip one of the famous ruby or tawny ports (aged tawny is especially good) or a Madeira dessert wine (Bual and Malvasia).

MADEIRA WINE

The history of the island's eponymous drink, famous the world over, is as full and well-rounded as a bottle of the best vintage Malvasia. When the island was first settled during the fifteenth century, Prince Henry ordered Zarco to plant vines, brought to the island from Crete. Although wine was not planned as a major export, it became one of the most important products of the island, thanks to a combination of its notable quality and Madeira's position on the shipping lanes to the East and West Indies. The island was an obvious stopping point, where water, fresh food and wine could be taken on-board. With the rise of the British colonies in North America and the West Indies, Madeira wine was soon established as a favourite on both sides of the Atlantic, and shipped all over the British Empire.

Initially, Madeira was not a fortified wine, but gradually the addition of grape brandy became common practice in order to stabilise it on long sea voyages. During the eighteenth century, it was discovered that shipping the wine actually improved its longevity as well as its flavour. Producers realised that tropical heat was the key ingredient, and towards the end of the century, pipes of Madeira were loaded as ballast on transatlantic journeys in order to 'cook' them as much as possible. When it became impractical to send barrels on return trips, conditions for heating the wine had to be reproduced at home. The easiest way was simply to store barrels in lofts that soaked up abundant sunlight. Subsequently, special tanks called *estufas*, centrally heated by hot-water pipes, were employed; this system is still in use today for cheaper Madeira wines, subjecting the wine to a temperature of 35°C (95°F) for six months.

Oxidisation during the heating process renders the wine virtually indestructible. A bottle of Madeira can be kept uncorked for many months without suffering any deterioration, even when other types of fortified wine (such as port) would moulder quickly under such conditions. For this reason, there are Madeira wines from the early 1800s that are entirely drinkable today.

Choosing a bottle. There are several types of Madeira, each named after the grape that gives that style of wine its distinctive flavour and characteristics. The lightest and driest is Sercial, which has a full-bodied, nutty flavour, not unlike an *amontillado* sherry. It is best served chilled as an aperitif. Verdelho and Terrantez are both classified as medium-dry and should be served slightly chilled. These are tangy aperitifs, and are also recommended as an accompaniment to soup.

Aged bottles of Madeira wine

Bual, probably introduced by the Jesuits in the seventeenth century, is a rich, port-like Madeira with a splendid honeyed taste and an underlying acidity, which means that it can cut through sweet desserts and is also a good accompaniment to cheese. Finally, and most famously, Malvasia (also known as Malmsey) is the richest of all, and is usually served following a meal.

Some Madeira wines are made from blends of several years, and the skill and style of the blender is what gives the wines of different shippers their individual character. The youngest component of the blend gives the stated age of the wine on the label: Finest is a blend in which the youngest is at least 3 years old, while Reserve and Special Reserve wines are at least 5 and 10 years old, respectively. The best, however, are Vintage wines, bottled after ageing in oak casks for a minimum of 20 years.

If you really want to impress your friends back home, buy a 75ml bottle of 1875 D'Oliveiras Malvasia Madeira Family Reserve for a mere €1,000 or so. If your budget doesn't stretch to that, you can pick up more recent vintages for around €20.

OTHER ISLAND DRINKS

After Madeira, the most famous drink produced on the island is *aguardente*, a powerful sugar cane distillation, which varies in taste from virtually unpalatable firewater to smooth, aged brandy. Look for the term *velha* (old) on the label unless you have an iron constitution. Add lemon juice and honey to *aguardente* and you have *poncha*, a delicious drink that belies its ferocious base.

Other liqueurs are distilled from the island's fruit, two notable examples being a cherry brandy from Curral das Freiras called *ginja*; and *licor de maracujá*, passion fruit liqueur (don't confuse it with the soft drink, *refrigerante de maracujá*). The local Coral lager (*cerveja*) is also excellent and very welcome on a hot day.

LIQUID HISTORY

It was Shakespeare who first gave Madeira wine a literary platform, when in *Henry IV* Falstaff is accused of selling his soul for a leg of chicken and a goblet of Madeira. The real Henry IV actually died before the discovery of the island, let alone the wine. In 1478, the Duke of Clarence went one better than Falstaff and actually drowned in a barrel of Malmsey. Sir Winston Churchill was once presented with a bottle of 1792 Sercial in Reid's Hotel, then delighted his guests by placing a napkin over his arm and assuming the duties of waiter.

But Madeira wine didn't win favour with just the British. It was used to toast the American Declaration of Independence, and drunk at the Inauguration of George Washington, who was said to consume a pint of Madeira at dinner daily. Benjamin Franklin and Thomas Jefferson were also Madeira connoisseurs.

TO HELP YOU ORDER

We'd like a table. **Queríamos uma mesa**.
I'd like a/an/some … **Queria** …

bread **pão**

rice **arroz**

butter **manteiga**

salad **salada**

coffee **um café**

soup **sopa**

dessert **sobremesa**

sugar **açucar**

fish **peixe**

tea **chá**

fruit **fruta**

wine **vinho**

ice cream **gelado**

meat **carne**

milk **leite**

fried **frito**

potatoes **batatas**

grilled **grelhado**

MENU READER

alho garlic

amêijoas baby clams

ananás pineapple

arroz rice

atum tuna

azeitonas olives

bacalhau cod (salted)

bife (vaca) steak (beef)

bolo cake

borrego lamb

camarões shrimps

caranguejo crab

cebola onion

chouriço spicy sausage

coelho rabbit

cogumelos mushrooms

feijões beans

figos figs

frango chicken

gambas prawns

guisado stew

laranja orange

legumes vegetables

linguado sole

lulas squid

maçã apple

mariscos shellfish

melancia watermelon

mexilhões mussels

molho sauce

ovo egg

pimento pepper

porco pork

presunto ham

queijo cheese

robalo sea bass

WHERE TO EAT

We have used the following symbols to give an idea of the price for a three-course meal for one, including wine, cover and service:

€€€€   **over 50 euros**
€€€   **30–50 euros**
€€   **20–30 euros**
€   **below 20 euros**

FUNCHAL TOWN

Armazém do Sal €€€ *Rua da Alfândega 135; tel: 291 241 285;* www.armazem-dosal.com. An unusual setting in a 400-year-old salt warehouse. Look out for the coat of arms by the door as this place isn't easy to find. A dark, rustic space, with plenty of fish and Portuguese wine on the menu. Open Mon–Fri for lunch and dinner, Sat dinner.

Restaurant do Forte €€€€ *Forte de São Tiago; tel: 291 215 580;* www.forte.restaurant. With a fantastic setting atop Funchal's mustard-yellow, seventeenth-century fort, some terrace tables here have views out to sea, peeking through the battlements. The menu includes pasta, risotto, grilled fish, and dishes such as duck with sweet potato cannelloni. Open daily for lunch and dinner.

Restaurante Informal €€€€ *Rua Murcas 39; tel: 924 253 293.* In the heart of the city next to the Cathedral, this cosy restaurant produces comfort food based around amazing flavour, using seasonal ingredients of the highest quality. The weekly changing three-course set lunch is great value and very popular. Tables are set up outside on the quiet street. Open Mon–Sat for lunch and dinner.

Londres €€ *Rua da Carreira; tel: 291 235 329.* A local favourite, this is a simple place serving simple dishes, of which the stand out is the grilled fish. Open Mon–Sat for lunch and dinner.

Marina Terrace €€€ *Marina do Funchal; tel: 291 230 547;* www.marinaterrace.pt. At the far end of the marina, this popular choice has a wide menu, but is particularly good for fish, shellfish, and steak, which is served sizzling on a hot slab. Open Mon–Sat for lunch and dinner.

Mozart €€€€ *Rua Don Carlos I; tel: 291 244 239; www.mozart.restaurant*. This attractive place in the old town has walls painted in snooker-green and hung with paintings, and the maitre d' is dressed in eighteenth-century costume. Food is sophisticated and there is regular live music. Open Mon–Sat for lunch and dinner.

O Tapassol €€ *62, Rua D. Carlos I; tel: 291 225 023*. In a characterful old building, decked with beautiful flowers, this establishment offers excellent, good-value local cuisine, including exceptional grilled fish. There is a great view from the terrace – book ahead for an outdoor table. Open daily for lunch and dinner.

Riso €€€ *Rua de Santa Maria 274; tel: 291 280 360*. This acclaimed gem provides amazing views of the ocean from its clifftop location, with alfresco dining being the best option – tables are set under a modernist white canopy. A wide choice of rice dishes from around the world, and plenty of options for vegetarians. Open Tues–Sun for lunch and dinner.

Taberna Madeira €€ *Travessa João Caetano 16; tel: 291 221 789*; www.tabernamadeira.net. Prepare to be wooed by this rustic setting, which features straw-like runners on the walls and ceiling as well as woven chairs. The menu is a mix of traditional recipes, with the tuna belly, octopus and pan-fried calves' liver among the must-tries. Open Mon–Sat for lunch and dinner, Sun dinner.

FUNCHAL HOTEL ZONE

Casal da Penha €€€ *Rua de Penha de França 1; tel: 291 227 674*; www.casaldapenha.com. This family-run restaurant perfectly showcases simple, regional specialities through a menu that lets the ingredients do the talking. The modest yet neat dining room is enhanced by a beautiful flower-filled roof terrace. Open Mon–Sat for lunch and dinner and Sun dinner.

Casa Velha €€€ *Rua Imperatriz Dona Amélia 69; tel: 291 205 600;* www.casavelharestaurant.com. A formal garden-like restaurant with bamboo chairs, ferns and ceiling fans, the 'Old House' has a nineteenth-century colonial feel. The short Madeiran and international menu is popular with nearby hotel guests. Piano bar downstairs. Open daily for lunch and dinner.

Dining Room €€€€ *Rua da Casa Branca 7; tel: 291 700 770*; www.quintacasa-branca.pt. This sophisticated restaurant serves creative and beautifully plated dishes in elegant surroundings. Dress code. Open daily for dinner.

Dona Amélia €€€ *Rua Imperatriz Dona Amélia 83; tel: 291 225 784;* www.do-naameliarestaurant.com. This chic upstairs restaurant is a good place for a romantic dinner of *espetadas* (kebabs), grilled fish, nice salads and soups. Open daily for dinner.

Ristorante Villa Cipriani €€€€ *Estrada Monumental 139 (in Belmond Reid's Palace Hotel); tel: 291 717 171;* www.belmond.com. Reid's elegant restaurant is widely praised for its excellent Italian cuisine and impeccable service. The open-air terrace offers unrivalled views over Funchal and the bay. Open Thurs–Mon for dinner.

Uva €€€€ *Rua dos Aranhas 27 (in the Vine Hotel); tel: 291 009 000;* www.hotel-thevine.com. This super-stylish restaurant in the boutique Vine Hotel serves up creative cuisine in a sleek, modernist setting, with huge plate-glass windows and a great terrace making the most of fantastic views. There's an extensive wine list. Open daily for dinner.

FUNCHAL TOURIST ZONE

Il Gallo d'Oro €€€€ *Cliff Bay Hotel, Estrada Monumental 147; tel: 291 707 700;* www.portobay.com. Two–Michelin-starred restaurant that serves extremely sophisticated Mediterranean and Iberian cuisine under the stewardship of chef Benoît Sinthon. Open Tues–Sat for dinner.

Tokos €€€€ *Estrada Monumental 169; tel: 291 771 019.* A tiny restaurant with an eccentric chef/owner (Felipe dos Ramos), this intimate place (just 10 or so tables) does everything well, but when the chef wheels out the trolley of fresh fish, you will be hard-pressed to order anything else. Excellent desserts and a very good wine cellar. Reservations essential. Open Mon–Sat for lunch and dinner and Sun dinner.

BEYOND FUNCHAL

Adega do Pomar €€€ *Rua Maria Ascensão, Camacha; tel: 938 799 379*; https://quintadamoscadinha.com. Located in Quinta da Moscadinha, this rustic restaurant serves beautifully cooked and presented traditional food in an old Madeiran tavern setting. Wine barrels and other typical props provide warmth to a cosy space. Open daily for lunch and dinner.

Restaurant Caravela €€ *Estrada Regional 101, São Vicente; tel: 291 842 814*. On the avenue right by the ocean, sea views can be enjoyed while tucking into simple and tasty Portuguese cuisine that focuses on fresh fish and shellfish. There are sweets made in the house and a good wine list with various options of Madeiran wines. Open daily for lunch and dinner.

Casa Velha do Palheiro €€€€ *Rua da Estalagem 23–São Gonçalo–Funchal; tel: 291 790 350*; www.palheironatureestate.com. The refined dining room in the grounds of the Quinta do Palheiro is one of the island's most elegant restaurants. Exquisite international and Portuguese dishes. Daily fixed-price and à la carte menus are available. Superb service and wine list. Open daily for dinner.

O Cesto €€ *Camacha; tel: 291 922 068*. This simple neighbourhood Camacha restaurant, with attached bar, is spacious and inviting, and serves good-value, home-style cooking, specialising in chicken and roasted meats. Open noon–4pm. Closed Thurs.

Orca €€€ *Rotunda das Piscinas 4, Porto Moniz, 9270-095; tel: 291 850 000*. This seaside restaurant has big windows and a terrace, both with fantastic views over the sea. The menu offers more of a seafood theme, with fresh grilled fish and shellfish dishes. Open daily 10am–6pm.

Praça do Engenho €€ *Rua da Praia, Porto da Cruz; tel: 291 563 680*. The *engenho* of this restaurant's name refers to the location on the seafront at Porta da Cruz, inside the converted engine room of a former sugar mill. Grey basalt walls lit by modern plate glass provide the setting for a leisurely meal of fresh seafood, which you can choose for yourself from a selection laid out on a bed of ice. Open daily 8am–11pm.

Quinta do Furão €€€ *Achada do Gramacho, Santana; tel: 291 570 100;* www. quintadofurao.com. This rustic restaurant, part of the hotel of the same name, serves some of the finest food on the entire north coast. Surrounded by orchards and a vineyard, it offers the freshest selection of local ingredients and seafood. Open daily for lunch and dinner.

Restaurante Ribeiro Frio €€ *Ribeiro Frio; tel: 291 575 898.* A cosy bar reminiscent of an English pub leads to a chalet-like dining area with a fireplace, and there's a greenery-surrounded terrace. Grilled trout, plucked fresh from the hatchery across the road, is the house speciality. Open daily 9am–6pm.

PORTO SANTO

Panorama Restaurant €€€ *Estrada Carlos Pestana Vasconcelos, Casinhas; tel: 966 789 680;* www.panorama-restaurante.pt. Set on a hilltop in one of the most fantastic spots on the island, wall-to-wall windows offer a stunning panoramic view of the entire island. From the kitchen come meat and fish dishes of great quality, such as grilled lamb chops in peppermint sauce or cod 'Panorama Style'. Open daily 6.30–11pm.

TRAVEL ESSENTIALS

PRACTICAL INFORMATION

A

ACCOMMODATION (see also Recommended hotels and Camping)

The government grades hotels and hotel-apartments (*aparthotels*) in Madeira from two to five stars. Below the rating of hotel is *estalagem*, which loosely translates as 'inn'. These may be simple hotels away from the main tourist areas, or they may be extremely comfortable, individually owned inns. The categories below *estalagem* are *albergaria, residência* and *pensão* – usually small bed-and-breakfast hotels with basic facilities, although a handful of *estalagens* and *albergarias* are the equivalent of five-star hotels.

Madeira is unique in also offering *quinta* accommodation. *Quintas* are gracious mansions and villas, usually set in splendid gardens, brimming with antiques and restored to provide a standard of accommodation (and prices) equivalent to a four- or five-star hotel. They do not offer all the sports or facilities and amenities of a top hotel, but in terms of character and personal service they are often much better. All are limited in the number of rooms, so book early. Early booking is also recommended if you want to stay on the island during the winter season between Christmas and New Year's Eve (see page 84).

Travellers familiar with Portugal might arrive in Madeira looking for a *pousada*, a luxury government-owned hotel set in a building of architectural and historical character. Madeira does not have any official *pousadas*, but there are privately run hotels that fits the general *pousada* principal, enjoying a tranquil, scenic setting away from the main tourist areas.

I'd like a single/double room with bath/shower. **Queria um quarto simples/duplo com banho/chuveiro.**
What's the rate per night? **Qual é o preço por noite?**

AIRPORTS

Madeira's Aeroporto Internacional da Madeira Cristiano Ronaldo (tel: 291 520 700; www.aeroportomadeira.pt/en/fnc/home) is in Santa Cruz, 22km (14 miles) east of Funchal. It used to have one of the shortest passenger runways in Europe until it was enlarged in 2000. Even so, arriving is still an adventure, and occasionally, in really bad weather, flights have to be diverted to Porto Santo.

From the airport to Funchal it is about 35 minutes by taxi or an hour by bus. During rush hour, double the time. Visitors can either take the city bus (€3.35), with multiple stops, the Aero bus (€5; €8 return) or a taxi, which has posted set fares (between €30 and €40 depending on the time of day) to Funchal's tourist or hotel zone, or city centre. Several car-hire agencies have desks at the airport, and there is a small tourist information kiosk, bureau de change, restaurant and bar. For bus schedules, see the website of SAM transport company (www.sam.pt).

There are frequent daily flights from Madeira to the airport at **Porto Santo** (tel: 291 980 122; www.aeroportoportosanto.pt/en/pxo/home). Direct flights to Porto Santo from Madeira are operated by Binter Canarias (www.bintercanarias.com). TAP Air Portugal (www.flytap.com) offers flights via Lisbon. There are also direct flights to Porto Santo from other countries or with connection through Lisbon and Oporto.

B

BICYCLE HIRE

You can rent a mountain bike from **Bike Zone** (tel: 291 756 241; www.bikezone.pt) at Rua Vale da Ajuda 100 in Funchal.

Where can I get a taxi? **Onde posso encontrar um táxi?**
How much is it to central Funchal? **Quanto custa para ir ao centro de Funchal?**
Does this bus go to Funchal? **Vai para Funchal este autocarro?**

BUDGETING FOR YOUR TRIP

Getting to Madeira. There are regular scheduled and charter flights direct to Madeira (or via Lisbon) from many European cities. Return flights from London are likely to cost from £100–400. Affordable package deals – flights and hotel included – are usually available.

Accommodation. Hotels at the top levels are comparable to those in large European cities. Many of the two-, three- and four-star ratings are relatively good value for money. A double room with bath per night in a cheaper hotel averages at around the €80–130 price mark; mid-range hotels charge roughly €130–180; while more luxurious and higher-end options can cost from €180 upwards.

Meals. Even top-rated restaurants may be surprisingly affordable compared to most European capitals. Portuguese wines are quite good and very attractively priced, even in fine restaurants. A three-course meal with wine in a reasonable establishment averages €20–50 per person. Many hotels offer half- and full-board plans.

Local transport. Buses and taxis are reasonably priced here. A bus to the centre of Funchal from the hotel or tourist zone is priced at around €2; if you plan on using the bus service regularly while you are on holiday, you can purchase a rechargeable Flexicard (ten trip minimum); a taxi costs roughly €5 (add a fare supplement of 20 percent on weekends and public holidays between 9pm and 7am).

Incidentals. Your major expenses will be excursions, entertainment and sporting activities. Hiring a car allows greater flexibility, although if you enter the interior you will have to contend with challenging roads and steep ascents and descents. Economy hire costs from €40–60 a day, including collision insurance and taxes. Petrol costs at around €1.75 a litre, and diesel is priced at around €1.55.

Nightclub cover charges can be high, and folklore or *fado* shows, including dinner, run at €23–60 per person.

Coach trips around the island from Funchal cost roughly €20–40. Island-hopping to Porto Santo by air is priced at about €60 return; by ferry, €57 return.

C

CAMPING

There are two official campsites on the Madeira archipelago, one in Porto Moniz (tel: 291 853 856) and the other on Porto Santo, in Vila Baleira. For more details contact: **Parque de Campismo do Porto Santo** (Vila Baleira, 9400 Porto Santo, Madeira; tel: 291 982 160) or visit www.madeiracamping.com. There are other wild camping areas on the island, but it is necessary to apply for permission from the Institute of Forests and Nature Conservation (tel: 291 145 590; email: ifcn@madeira.gov.pt).

Is there a campsite near here? **Há algum parque de campismo por aqui perto?**
May we camp here? **Podemos acampar aqui?**

CAR HIRE (see also Driving and Budgeting for your trip)

There are local and international car hire agencies in Funchal (most near the hotel and tourist zones) and at the airport. Prices vary significantly, so shop around – local firms tend to be cheaper and less prone to charging extra for scratches or dents.

You must be at least 21 and have held a valid national (or international) licence for at least a year. You need to present a recognised credit card when booking. Third party fire and theft insurance is included in the basic charge. Check with your credit-card company before departure to verify what it covers when used to pay for the rental. Many will cover the collision damage waiver and theft of vehicle protection; when booking locally a government tax will be added to the total bill.

An economy hire (such as a Nissan Micra) starts at €170 per week. Major international agents are: **Avis** (Largo António Nobre 164; tel: 291 764 546); **Eu-**

ropcar (Estrada Monumental 306; tel: 291 765 116); **Hertz** (Cristiano Ronaldo Airport; tel: 291 426 300); and **Sixt** (Estrada Monumental 182; tel: 255 788 199).

> I'd like to hire a car **Queria alugar um carro**
> … tomorrow **… para amanhã**
> … for one day/one week. **… por um dia/uma semana.**
> Please include full insurance. **Que inclua um seguro contra todos os riscos, por favor.**

CLIMATE

Madeira is generally warm and spring-like all year, making it an excellent winter retreat for northern Europeans. However, winter months can be rather wet and windy. The rainiest period is from October to December, with an average of six to seven days of rain per month, but you can usually count on an average of six hours sunshine each day. From May to September, the air is warm and somewhat humid. The typical pattern, year-round, is a clear, bright morning, with clouds rolling down from the mountains in the afternoon. For warm, clear weather, ideal for mountain walking, summer is your best bet. Average daily temperatures are:

	J	F	M	A	M	J	J	A	S	O	N	D
min												
°C	13	13	13	14	16	17	19	19	19	18	16	14
°F	56	56	56	58	60	63	66	67	67	65	61	58
max												
°C	19	18	19	19	21	22	24	24	24	23	22	19
°F	66	65	66	67	69	72	75	76	76	74	71	67

CLOTHING

Light clothes are all you need in summer, but pack warm layers for mountain excursions. In winter a light, rainproof jacket may come in handy and you will definitely need warm, waterproof clothes for inland trips. If you are planning on walking you will obviously need sensible footwear, but unless you are intent on tackling some of the more arduous trails, you won't need hiking boots.

Madeira has long been a place where visitors dress up for tea and formal dinners. There is less formality these days – shorts and T-shirts are fine during the day – but at some luxury hotels and restaurants jacket and tie are generally expected (enquire about dress code when booking). Nightspots such as the casino are more relaxed and Jackets and ties are not required.

Will I need a tie? **É preciso gravata?**
Is it all right if I wear this? **Vou bem assim?**

CRIME AND SAFETY (see also Emergencies and police)

Although Madeira is one of the safest places in the world for tourists, factors such as poverty (which does exist here, especially in small villages) inevitably make temptation irresistible for some, and there have been some problems with drug users mugging walkers along lonely *levada* trails. Follow the same general rules that you would elsewhere. Never leave anything of value in your car, even if it is out of sight. Burglaries of holiday apartments are rare, but leave any valuables in a safe-deposit box, or, in a hotel, with reception staff. You must report any losses to the police within 24 hours and get a copy of your statement for insurance purposes.

I want to report a theft. **Quero participar um roubo.**

D

DRIVING

There are several good reasons not to drive on Madeira: car hire and petrol are not cheap, but taxis are, and the tortuous mountain roads can be hard on one's nerves. Conversely, you may enjoy the challenge of the winding roads and, of course, a car gives maximum flexibility.

Road conditions. It is only worth considering driving into Funchal if you are staying well outside the town (at Machico or Garajau, for instance). If you do, expect traffic jams. The roads across the island offer a choice between fast modern highways, often enclosed in tunnels, or scenic but slow mountain roads that can be torturously twisting. The latter demand confident, relaxed drivers.

Rules and regulations. The rules are the same as in the rest of continental Europe: drive on the right, overtake on the left, and give way to vehicles coming from the right. Speed limits are 100–120kph (62–75mph) on highways, 90kph (56mph) outside built-up areas and 40–50kph (25–30mph) in built-up areas. Average speeds on country roads are well below 60kph (37mph). Seat belts must be worn at all times and children under the age of 12 are not allowed in front seats. Motorcyclists must always wear helmets.

Fuel costs. Unleaded petrol is around €1.75 per litre, diesel is around €1.55. Prices, controlled by the government, should be the same – or very similar – everywhere you go. Many petrol stations are open 24 hours a day, and all accept credit cards.

If you need help. If you are driving a hired car, the hire company will give you a number to contact in case of breakdown or emergency. If you belong to a motoring organisation affiliated to the **Automóvel Clube de Portugal** (www.acp.pt), you can make use of its services free of charge. You will have no problem finding well-equipped garages in Madeira.

Parking. Funchal is served by reasonably priced car parks at either end of town. Parking in the centre is virtually impossible, except in the 'blue zone' (metered parking) along Avenida do Mar e das Comunidades Madeirenses (facing the Marina). You should have few difficulties parking elsewhere on the island.

Alto Stop
Cruzamento Crossroads
Curva perigosa Dangerous bend/curve
Descida íngreme Steep hill
Desvio Detour
Encruzilhada Crossing
Estacionamento permitido Parking permitted
Estacionamento proibido No parking
Guiar com cuidado Drive with care
Máquinas em manobras Men working
Obras/Trabalhos Men working
Paragem (de autocarro) Bus stop
Pare Stop
Pedestres, peões Pedestrians
Perigo Danger
Proibida a entrada No entry
Seguir pela direita/esquerda Keep right/left
Sem saída No through road
Are we on the right road for...? **É esta estrada para...?**
Fill it up, please, with... **Encha, por favor, de...**
three star/four star/unleaded/diesel **normal/super/sem
    chumbo/gasóleo**
My car's broken-down **O meu carro está avariado**
There's been an accident **H ouve um acidente**

E

ELECTRICITY

The standard current is 220-volt, 50Hz AC. For US appliances, 220v transformers and plug adaptors are needed.

I need an adaptor/a battery, please. **Preciso de um adaptador/ uma pilha, por favor.**

EMBASSIES AND CONSULATES

Embassies of the following nations are located in Lisbon at the following addresses:

UK (Embassy) Rua de São Bernardo 33, Lisbon; tel: 21 392 4000; www.gov.uk/world/organisations/british-embassy-lisbon.

Australia (Embassy) Avenida da Liberdade 200, Lisbon; tel: 21 310 1500; www.portugal.embassy.gov.au.

Canada (Embassy/Consulate) Avenida da Liberdade 198–200, 3°, Lisbon; tel: 21 316 4600; www.canadainternational.gc.ca/portugal.

Republic of Ireland (Embassy/Consulate) Avenida da Liberdade 200, 4th floor, Lisbon; tel: 21 330 8200; www.dfa.ie/irish-embassy/portugal.

South Africa (Embassy) Avenida Luís Bívar 10, Lisbon; tel: 21 319 2200; www.embaixada-africadosul.pt.

US (Embassy/Consulate) Avenida das Forças Armadas 16, Lisbon; tel: 21 727 3300; https://pt.usembassy.gov.

Where is the British embassy? **Onde é a embaixada inglesa?**

EMERGENCIES (see also Health and medical care)

The emergency number for police, fire or ambulance is the same. Dial **112** for either service.

Funchal hospital has a 24-hour emergency ward; tel: 291 705 600. Alternatively, outside of Funchal, you will need to ask for the local Centro de Saúde (Health Centre).

G

GETTING THERE (see also Airports)

Air Travel. There are frequent charter flights to Madeira from international and regional airports in the UK and from international airports all over Europe. The national Portuguese airline is TAP/Air Portugal (www.flytap.com), which flies from several European cities to Funchal, sometimes via Lisbon or Porto. For cheaper fares, check with easyJet (www.easyjet.com), for 'no-frills' flights to Funchal from London Gatwick, Bristol and Manchester. Regular flights are also operated by Jet2.com (www.jet2.com) from London Stansted, Bristol, Edinburgh, Glasgow, Leeds, Newcastle and Manchester. The flight time from London to Madeira is approximately 3 hours 30 minutes, and from Lisbon to Madeira about 1 hour 30 minutes.

Many charter flights connect Madeira to mainland Europe and are much less expensive. Cruise liners stop off at the island, but often only for a brief tour.

GUIDES AND TOURS (see Public transport)

A good way of seeing Madeira is by coach or minibus tour. Several operators go to the same places, but charge different rates for different services. Itineraries include: west of the Island; east of the Island, including Pico do Arieiro; a half-day covering Monte/Curral das Freiras/Pico dos Barcelos; guided *levada* walks; and Jeep safaris to out-of-the-way places such as Boca dos Namorados (see page 45) or Paúl da Serra (see page 50). Not all of these are good value; the Monte trip is simple and inexpensive to do by yourself (see page 41), as are the *levada* walks (see page 60). Other itineraries offer a day trip to Porto Santo, including an island tour (this is only recommended in summer, when sunshine and calm sailing are the norm), but you can also make your own way to the island and take a half-day minibus tour. Half-day boat trips cruise up and down the Madeiran coast, and other outings from Funchal Marina include a trip to the Ilhas Desertas, or a full day's sailing, including lunch and wine.

The tourist offices (see page 131) in Funchal – and most hotels – can provide information on tour operators, including Blandy's and other agencies. Particularly highly recommended are **Lido Tours** (Estrada Monumental 284; tel: 291 635 505), who offer small island minibus tours and *levada* and mountain walks; guides speak multiple languages and tours are good value.

Another recommended tour company is **Windsor Travel** (tel: 291 700 600; www.windsormadeira.com), which runs well-organised tours across the island, including to the viewing point at Pico dos Barcelos and to the island of Porto Santo.

Madeira Explorers focuses on guided outdoor ecotourism (Centro Commercial Monumental Experience, Shop 5, 3rd Floor; tel: 291 763 701; www.madeira-levada-walks.com). **Nature Meetings** specialises in guided walks, which you can do as part of a group, or individually, with transport provided at the start and end of the walk (tel: 291 524 482; www.naturemeetings.com). **Up Mountain Madeira** organises ridge and *levada* walks as well as Jeep safaris (Funchal, 9060-011 Madeira; tel: 925 964 335; www.upmountainmadeira.com).

We'd like an English-speaking guide/an English interpreter.
Queremos um guia que fale inglês/um intérprete de inglês.

H

HEALTH AND MEDICAL CARE (see also Emergencies)

There are numerous health centres in Madeira and one on Porto Santo. *Farmácias* (chemists) are open Monday through Friday 9am to 1pm, 3pm to 7pm, Saturdays 9am to 1pm. On the door of every pharmacy you will find postings of after-hours chemists.

Tourist offices carry lists of doctors and dentists who speak English. For more serious illness or injury, Hospital Dr Nélio Mendonça (Avenida Luis de

Camoes 57; tel: 291-705 600) is the island's largest hospital and has English-speaking staff. In an emergency, dial **112** for an ambulance.

It is highly recommended that you take out travel insurance to cover any costs associated with illness or accidents while abroad. EU and UK nationals with a European or Global Health Insurance Card (EHIC/GHIC), obtainable on-line at www.nhs.uk/using-the-nhs/healthcare-abroad, can receive free emergency treatment at Social Security and Municipal hospitals. Private hospitals are expensive. If you don't take the EHIC/GHIC card with you, you must pay on the spot and claim on your travel insurance later. Note that EHIC cards are valid until their expiry date. Once expired, you will need to apply for a GHIC as a replacement.

All visitors should check the latest Covid-19 vaccination protocol for Madeira before travelling.

Where's the nearest (all night) pharmacy? **Onde fica a farmácia (de serviço) mais próxima?**
I need a doctor/dentist **Preciso de um médico/dentista**
an ambulance **uma ambulância**
hospital **hospital**
An upset stomach **Dôr de estômago**
Sunburn/a fever **Queimadura de sol/febre**

The most likely health problems will be due to an excess of sun or alcohol. Madeiran tap water (*água*) is safe and tastes pretty good. Bottled mineral water is sold everywhere.

Mosquitoes are present in summer, so buy repellent or a plug-in device at the airport.

HOLIDAYS

1 January **Ano Novo** New Year's Day

25 April **Dia da Liberdade** Freedom Day
1 May **Dia do Trabalho** Labour Day
10 June **Dia de Portugal** National Day
1 July **Dia da Região Autónoma da Madeira e das Comunidades Madei-renses** Madeira Autonomous Region and Madeiran Communities Day
15 August **Assunção** Assumption
5 October **Dia da República** Republic Day
1 November **Todos os Santos** All Saints' Day
1 December **Dia da Restauração da Independência** Independence Restoration Day
8 December **Dia da Imaculada Conceição** Feast of the Immaculate Conception
25 December **Dia de Natal** Christmas Day
26 December **Dia de** Santo Estêvão St Stephen's Day (Boxing Day)
Movable dates:
Terça-feira Gorda/Carnaval Shrove Tuesday/Carnival
Sexta-feira Santa Good Friday
Domingo de Páscoa Easter Sunday
Corpo de Cristo Corpus Christi

L

LANGUAGE

Madeira's official language is Portuguese. Basic Spanish should help with reading signs and menus, but is unlikely to unlock the mysteries of spoken Portuguese.

The pocket-size Rough Guides Phrasebook Portuguese (Bilingual dictionary), should cover most situations you are likely to encounter during a visit to Portugal.

LGBTQ TRAVELLERS

www.portugalgay.pt features a LGBTQ travel guide, with information in English and other languages. It has little specific information relating to Madeira,

Good day/afternoon/evening **Bom dia/Boa tarde/Boa noite**
Goodbye **Adeus**
please **faz favor/por favor**
thank you **obrigado/obrigada (male/female speaker)**
How do you do/Pleased to meet you **Muito prazer**
How are you? **Como está?**
Very well, thank you **Muito bem, obrigado/obrigada**
What does this mean? **Que quer dizer isto?**
Please write it down **Escreva-mo, por favor**
where/when/how? **onde/quando/como?**
how long/how far? **quanto tempo/a que distância?**
left/right **esquerdo/direito**
cheap/expensive **barato/caro**
hot/cold **quente/frio**
old/new **velho/novo**
open/closed **aberto/fechado**
vacant/occupied **livre/ocupado**
early/late **cedo/tarde**
Help me, please **Ajude-me, por favor**
day/week/month/year **dia/semana/mês/ano**
yesterday/today/tomorrow **ontem/hoje/amanhã**
Sunday **domingo**
Monday **segunda-feira**
Tuesday **terça-feira**
Wednesday **quarta-feira**
Thursday **quinta-feira**
Friday **sexta-feira**
Saturday **sábado**
What day is it today? **Que dia é hoje?**

but there is a message board for postings.

M

MAPS

Madeira is a small island with relatively few roads, so orientation is easy. The tourist offices in Funchal and Porto Santo can supply a free map that includes the island and capital and shows several of the most popular *levada* trails. For almost all purposes, even driving across the whole island, the free map should be sufficient, but more detailed maps are published by the Instituto Geográfico e Cadastral, obtainable at local bookshops.

Few maps are up to date because of the rapid pace of road building. The best map available in the UK is the Madeira Tour and Trail Map. Those intent on serious walking should buy a copy of *Landscapes of Madeira* by John and Pat Underwood (Sunflower Books; www.sunflowerbooks.co.uk), which includes specially drawn walking tour maps and details many *levada* trails. Their *Walk & Eat Madeira* series is aimed at those on shorter trips, but also contains detailed walking trails.

MEDIA

Europe's principal papers, including most British daily papers, are on the newsstands the day after publication. Popular foreign magazines are sold at many kiosks. Two useful online publications are the *Madeira Live* (www.madeira-live.com) and the Madeira Web (www.madeira-web.com), which provide information on weather, transport, events and local news. *Essential Madeira* (www.essential-madeira.com) is a glossy lifestyle magazine, available both online and in print. If you can understand a little Portuguese, the daily *Notícias da Madeira* (www.dnoticias.pt) newspaper gives you a weather forecast and details of museum and temporary exhibitions, among other things.

Madeira has its own TV channel and also receives programmes from mainland Portugal. Most large hotels and some bars also have satellite TV for screening football matches and other sporting events.

The BBC World Service and Voice of America can be heard on shortwave radio.

Have you any English-language newspapers/magazines? **Tem jornais/revistas em inglês?**

MONEY (see also Budgeting for your trip)

Currency. The euro is the official currency used in Portugal. Notes are denominated in 5, 10, 20, 50, 100 and 500 euros; coins in 1 and 2 euros and 1, 2, 5, 10, 20 and 50 cents.

Currency exchange. Normal banking hours are Monday to Friday from 8.30am to 3pm. Some banks remain open later and at weekends to change money. There is also a 24-hour bureau de change at the airport. Banks either levy up to 12 percent in commission or charge a minimum fee of €8, regardless of the amount, so ask first. ATMs are the easiest method of obtaining euros and provide by far the best exchange rates.

Credit cards. Standard international credit cards are widely accepted, except in some shops and restaurants, especially in small villages.

Can I pay with this credit card? **Posso pagar com cartão de crédito?**
I want to change some pounds/dollars. **Queria trocar libras/ dólares.**
Can you cash a traveller's cheque? **Pode pagar um cheque de viagem?**
Where's the nearest bank/ currency exchange office? **Onde fica o banco mais próximo/a casa de câmbio mais próxima?**
How much is that? **Quanto custa isto?**

O

OPENING HOURS

Most businesses close for a one- to two-hour lunch break. Shops and offices are generally open weekdays between 9am and 1pm and 3pm and 7pm, and from 9am to 1pm on Saturdays. Shopping centres and supermarkets open daily from 10am to 10pm. Banks are open between 8.30am and 3pm on weekdays, some also open on Saturdays between 9am–1pm. Currency exchange offices usually open between 9am and 1pm and 2pm and 7pm on weekdays, and until 1pm on Saturdays.

Museums are generally open Tuesday through Friday from 10am to 5pm, although some close between 12.30pm and 2pm, and some open at weekends, especially during summer. Café-restaurants may be open all day, whereas more up-market establishments tend to close after lunch and reopen for dinner.

P

POLICE (see also Emergencies)

The national police, identified by their blue uniforms, are generally helpful and friendly and often speak a little English. If you need assistance or find yourself in an emergency situation, dial 112. The main police station in Funchal, where there is a lost property section, is located on Rua da Infância 28 (tel: 291 208 400).

> Where's the nearest police station? **Onde fica o posto de polícia mais próximo?**
> I've lost… my wallet/bag/passport **Perdi... a minha carteira/o meu saco/o meu passaporte**

POST OFFICES (see also Telephones)

Post offices are indicated by the letters CTT (*Correios, Telégrafos e Telefones;* www.ctt.pt). Mailboxes are painted bright red for second-class post and blue (*Correio Azul*) for first-class and next day delivery post. Some post offices have separate slots for mail to the Portuguese mainland or international mail. The main post office in Funchal is on Avenida Zarco between Avenida Arriaga and Rua Carreira. It is open Monday through Saturday between 9am and 8pm. Local branches have shorter opening hours. You can buy stamps from tobacconists and kiosks, as well as at post offices.

Worldwide postage of a letter or postcard weighing up to 20g costs €0.83. Mail may take up to five days to reach a European destination.

Where's the nearest post office? **Onde fica a estação de correios mais próxima?**
express (special delivery) **expresso**
registered **registrado**

PUBLIC TRANSPORT

Buses. Most of the island is served by public buses, which are cheap, reliable and generally punctual. For those with the luxury of time and patience, it is possible to go almost anywhere that coach tours visit by public bus – a much cheaper but more time-consuming alternative. The tourist office sells a booklet giving details of bus services and routes. Bus stops are indicated by the sign *paragem*.

The three largest bus operators are SAM (www.sam.pt), Rodoeste (www.rodoeste.pt) and Horários do Funchal (www.horariosdofunchal.pt). They have their main departure points on the Avenida do Mar. You will find them between the Palácio de São Lourenço and the Zona Velha (Old Town).

Note that some intra-city and inter-city buses have identical numbers – for example, the orange town bus No. 20 to Monte is not the same as the green/

cream island bus No. 20 to Santo da Serra.

Bus companies in Funchal have introduced a Giro card system; the initial card can be purchased from automatic machines around the city or from authorised sellers and costs €0.50. These cards are rechargeable and need to be validated when you get on the bus. Various charges apply, depending on the number of zones travelled; the 15-day pass costs €22.50. Children under-6 travel free and those aged 6–16 qualify for reduced fares. SAM operates a different system of Flexicards which come in numerous categories (www.sam.pt/en/fares/113-flexicard-en.html).

Taxi. Metered taxis – which cannot be hailed in the street but are found at ranks all over Funchal and in every town – are reasonably priced and convenient for most trips within Funchal and to sights just outside the city, such as Monte, the Jardim Botânico and the Quinta do Palheiro. For many popular tourist trips, there is a government-set flat fare, which, by law, has to be displayed inside the taxi. Otherwise, the meter begins at €3.25 (€3.90 between 9pm and 6am, Sat, Sun and holidays). From the city centre to the hotel zone, expect to pay about €5. From the hotel zone to the airport costs around €30.

Many people hire taxis as substitutes for coach tours. If several people are travelling, this can be a good deal. Most taxis will charge about €60–80 per half day or €100–120 for a full day. A list of popular excursions and prices is

Where is the nearest bus stop? **Onde é a paragem de autocarros mais próxima?**
When's the next bus to ...? **Quando parte o próximo autocarro para...?**
I want a ticket to ... **Queria um bilhete para...**
single/return **ida/ida e volta**
Will you tell me when to get off? **Pode dizer-me quando devo descer?**
Where can I get a taxi? **Onde posso encontrar um táxi?**
What's the fare to...? **Quanto custa um bilhete para...?**

kept at the tourist office, or see Taxi Madeira (www.taximadeira.com).

Cable car. A cable car connects Funchal's Zona Velha (Old Town) to Monte, in the mountains above the city, and takes approximately fifteen minutes. Check opening hours and fares at www.telefericodofunchal.com.

Flights to Porto Santo. Porto Santo can be reached easily several times a day by small aircraft from Madeira airport (Binter Canarias; www.bintercanarias.com). Flight time approximately fifteen minutes, from about €65 return.

Ferry to Porto Santo. The Porto Santo Line (Avenida do Mar e das Comunidades Madeirenses; tel: 291 210 300; www.portosantoline.pt) operates a cruise-style ferry that departs from Funchal's harbour daily at 8am, and takes about two hours. It leaves Porto Santo at 7pm and costs around €55 return. In winter the timetable is slightly reduced. The new ships are far more stable than the old but travel pills are recommended for anyone prone to seasickness.

T

TELEPHONES

Portugal's country code is 351. Within Madeira, the local area code, 291, must always be dialled, even for local calls (check that the telephone number is nine digits in total).

A few Portugal Telecom public telephones take coins, but most accept only prepaid phonecards. Phonecards can be purchased at post offices or at newspaper kiosks. Local, national and international calls can also be made from hotels, but with a substantial surcharge. Use an international calling card if you must make a phone call from your hotel room.

A phone card, please. **Um credifone, por favor.**
Where's the pay phone? **Onde está o telefone pago?**
My phone doesn't work here. **O meu telefone não funciona aqui.**

To make an international call, dial 00 for an international line plus the country code (eg UK 0044, US 001) plus phone number (including the area code, without the initial '0' where there is one).

For directory enquiries in Madeira, dial 118, and 177 for international directory enquiries assistance.

Madeira has good mobile phone network coverage. If you are travelling from outside the EU (EU residents can 'roam like at home' until 2032), you should check mobile roaming charges with your service provider before you go to avoid any unpleasantly huge bills on your return. If your GSM phone is unlocked (which you can have done locally), you may use a local pay-as-you-go SIM card for cheaper local calls, which you can buy from provider networks Vodafone, MEO or NOS.

TIME

Madeira operates both winter (GMT + 0) and summer (GMT + 1) time periods, so Madeira is on the same time as the UK. From the last Sunday in March until the last Sunday in October, the clocks are moved one hour ahead. Times in summer are:

Sydney	**Madeira**	London	Los Angeles	New York
9pm	**noon**	noon	4am	7am

TIPPING

Hotel and restaurant bills are generally inclusive, but an additional tip of 5–10 percent is common and even expected in many restaurants across the island. Hotel wages are not high, and tips help to boost staff income: porters generally receive €1 a bag, the maid who cleans your room €1 a day. Taxi drivers do not expect a tip except for any special services.

TOILETS

Public toilets are rare in Funchal, and not usually recommended. The best

> Where are the toilets please? **¿Por favor, onde é o quarto de
> banho?**

place to find a clean toilet is in a large hotel, restaurant or bar (out of courtesy
you should buy a drink, or at least ask permission). 'Ladies' is marked *Senhoras*
and 'Gents' *Homens* or *Senhores*. *Senhoras* and *Senhores* are easily confused so
check carefully before entering.

TOURIST INFORMATION

Portugal does not have national tourist offices as such. Instead it main-
tains a website, Visit Portugal (www.visitportugal.com), from which various
brochures can be downloaded. In addition, Madeira has its own website –
Madeira Tourism (www.visitmadeira.pt) – with plenty of information. For
more information on Madeira tel: 966 765 718. This service is available daily,
between 9am and 8pm.

The Madeira Tourism Board operates nine offices on the archipelago, three in
Funchal and one on Porto Santo island. The most dependable is at Avenida Arria-
ga 16 in Funchal (tel: 291 145 305; info.srtc@madeira.gov.pt; Mon–Fri 9am–7pm,
Sat & Sun 9am–3.30pm). Provincial offices in Ponto del Sol, Ribeira Brava, Porto
Moniz, Santana and Porto Santo keep shorter hours and some close for lunch.
The airport tourist office (tel: 291 524 933) is open daily from 9am to 9.30pm.

V

VISAS AND ENTRY REQUIREMENTS

To visit Portugal, UK citizens, Americans, Canadians and many other nationali-
ties do not need a visa, just a passport valid for six months. EU citizens may enter
with an identity card. The length of stay authorised for most tourists is 90 days.

Before travelling to Madeira check official government websites or www.
visitmadeira.com for the latest Covid-19 pandemic updates, as restrictions
can change at a moment's notice.

Currency restrictions. Visitors from abroad may bring into Portugal (or depart with) any amount of euros or foreign currency.

Customs. Madeira is part of the EU, but has separate duty-free status within Portugal. Visitors from outside the EU can import the following amounts duty-free: 200 cigarettes, 50 cigars or 250g of tobacco; 1 litre of spirits; 4 litres of wine; 50g of perfume and 250ml of eau de toilette.

W

WEBSITES

www.apmadeira.pt Informative site with links to hotels, restaurant and other useful tourist providers.

www.madeira-web.com Run by a commercial travel agent, in English, German, Spanish and Portuguese, with a guide to outdoor activities, island tours and property.

www.visitmadeira.pt A helpful destination-specific site packed with lots of up-to-date travel information and advice, published by the Madeira Board of Tourism.

www.madeiraapartments.com A guide to self-catering accommodation on Madeira as an alternative to hotels.

Y

YOUTH HOSTELS

There are a limited number of official youth hostels in Madeira. Two in Funchal worth trying can be found on Avenida Calouste Gulbenkian (tel: 291 741 540) and Rua de Santa Maria (tel: 291 649 120). Around the island other good options include Sítio dos Serrões Acima in Calheta (tel: 291 822 500) and at Vila do Porto Moniz in Porto Moniz (tel: 291 853 915).

A modern hostel in Santana on Rua Tenente Domingos Cardoso (tel: 291 573 090) is the island's most recent facility.

Visit the website of the International Youth Hostelling Federation at www.hihostels.com for further information.

WHERE TO STAY

The choice of hotel accommodation on Madeira is wider than ever. Traditional hotels are clustered in the hotel and tourist zones hugging the coast west of Funchal. Many of these have been updating their design and services to compete with newer hotels in the *zona turista*. At the same time, hotel accommodation across the island is rapidly being expanded, and visitors can choose from hotels, *quintas* (villas) and *estalagens* along the coast and in the villages and mountains of the interior.

Book especially early for Christmas and New Year (when most hotels charge a huge supplement) and for smaller hotels throughout the year. Otherwise, high season rates generally apply from Easter, through May and July, to the end of September. Price guidelines below are for a double room with bath in high season, including breakfast and VAT (value-added tax). All hotels accept major credit cards. For making reservations, Portugal's country code is 351; the area code, 291, is the same throughout Madeira and must always be dialled.

€€€€	over 200 euros
€€€	150–200 euros
€€	100–150 euros
€	below 100 euros

FUNCHAL TOWN

Castanheiro Boutique Hotel €€ *Rua do Castanheiro 31, 9000-081 Funchal; tel: 291 200 100;* www.castanheiroboutiquehotel.com. Good-value accommodation in an excellent location just off Praça do Município. Some of the well-equipped rooms have a kitchenette, and there is a lap pool with panoramic views. 81 rooms and suites.

Porto Santa Maria €€ *Avenida do Mar e das Comunidades Madeirenses 50, 9060-190 Funchal; tel: 291 206 700;* www.portobay.com. Located on the seafront in the Old Town, close to the cable car and next door to the seventeenth-century São Tiago fortress. Comfortable, refurbished rooms. Studio apartments also available. There is a heated indoor pool, restaurant and two bars to make the most of. Access available for travellers with disabilities. 146 rooms.

Quinta da Bela Vista €€€€ *Caminho do Avista Navios 4, 9000 Funchal; tel: 291 706 400; www.belavistamadeira.com.* A plush hotel at the eastern end of the Old Town, built around an elegant nineteenth-century mansion, with splendid views and a lovely garden. The beautiful rooms are furnished with antiques. Excellent food at the formal restaurant. Small gym and sauna, swimming pool and library. 89 rooms.

Turim Santa Maria €€ *Rua João de Deus 26, 9050 Funchal; tel: 210 514 720; www.turim-hotels.com/turim-santa-maria-hotel-pt.* Chic, contemporary hotel in the Old Town, close to some excellent restaurants. Rooftop swimming pool with views over Funchal. 92 rooms.

Windsor €€ *Rua das Hortas 4, 9050 Funchal; tel: 291 233 081; www.hotelwindsorgroup.pt.* Hotel Windsor Group is a chain of three hotels located in the centre of Funchal: The Windsor Hotel, Hotel do Centro and Residencial Greco. They have all been beautifully refurbished and are a good choice for those who want to be housed in the heart of the city. 67 rooms.

FUNCHAL HOTEL ZONE

Aparthotel Imperatriz € *Rua da Imperatriz Dona Amélia 72, 9000 Funchal; tel: 291 233 456; www.hotel-imperatriz.com.* Surrounded by luxury hotels, and adjacent to the casino, these studio apartments, all with kitchenette and balcony, have a rooftop swimming pool with views of the sea. A good choice for those on a tight budget. 27 studios.

Avenue Park Apartamentos Turísticos € *Avenida do Infante 26, 9000 Funchal; tel: 291 205 630.* Smart, modern apartments (studios and one- and two-bedroom apartments) fashionably equipped with modern furnishings in bright colours and nice, clean kitchenettes. Located across from the Santa Catarina Park and the casino, and no more than a five-minute walk from Funchal's city centre. Access available for travellers with disabilities. 15 apartments.

NEXT hotel €€€ *Rua Carvalho Araújo 8, 9000-022 Funchal; tel: 291 205 700;* www.hotelnext.pt. Spacious and well-equipped rooms, suites and apartments with sun terraces and access to the sea. Indoor and captivating rooftop infinity pool. Most rooms overlook the sea and harbour. The staff are exceptionally friendly. Facilities include a gym and spa. Access available for travellers with disabilities. 166 rooms and suites.

Penha de França €€ *Rua da Imperatriz Dona Amélia 85, 9000 Funchal; tel: 291 204 650;* www.penhafranca.com. A restored manor house (*albergaria*) tucked away in a lovely garden in the midst of Funchal's hotel district. Although small and intimate, it nevertheless has a piano bar, outdoor dining, a lawn and a pool with an expansive terrace and terrific sea views. Stylish and modern rooms are aplenty here. Access available for travellers with disabilities. 109 rooms.

Pestana Carlton Madeira €€€€ *Largo António Nobre 1, 9000 Funchal; tel: 291 239 500;* www.pestana.com. Luxurious five-star clifftop complex overlooking Funchal Bay. The hotel spans a river gorge with direct views of the sea. Rooms are spacious and comfortable, and all have balconies. Four restaurants and lively nightlife, as well as a spa, two swimming pools, diving school and other sports facilities. Package deals are available. Access available for travellers with disabilities. 375 rooms.

Pestana Casino Park €€€ *Rua da Imperatriz Dona Amélia 55, 9000 Funchal; tel: 291 209 100;* www.pestana.com. Large 1960s concrete complex (designed by the great Brazilian architect Oscar Niemeyer) set within its own gardens overlooking the coast and Funchal's harbour. It offers a large swimming pool, activities and nightly entertainment at the adjacent casino and nightclubs. The tastefully furnished rooms all have balconies. Slightly less expensive than competing five-star hotels. Access available for travellers with disabilities. 379 rooms.

Pestana CR7 €€€ *Av. Sá Carneiro/Praça do Mar, 9000-017 Funchal; tel: 291 140 480;* www.pestanacr7.com. Opened in 2016 as a joint venture between Cristiano Ronaldo and the Pestana hotel group, this hotel is a high-tech marvel with soundproof windows, high-speed Wi-Fi and Apple TV, as well as Bluetooth audio, HDMI connections and motion-sensitive LED lights. Facilities include an outdoor pool, a gym, Jacuzzi and sauna. A rooftop bar, where parties often take place, and the more formal CR7 Funchal Lounge restaurant make good dining options. Excellent breakfast included. Guests get free tickets to the adjacent CR7 Museum. 82 rooms.

Quinta Perestrello €€€ *Rua Dr Pita 3, 9000 Funchal; tel: 291 706 700;* www.quintaperestrellomadeira.com. Delightful 150-year-old country house with period antiques, a lovely garden and swimming pool. Located close to Quinta do Magnolia park, but adjacent to a busy road junction, some rooms can be subject to traffic noise. The restaurant serves light meals, but guests can avail of all the facilities at sister hotels in the Charming Hotels Madeira group. 36 rooms.

Royal Savoy €€€€ *Rua Carvalho Araújo, 9000 Funchal; tel: 291 213 500;* www. savoysignature.com. The luxurious five-star Royal Savoy is situated in Funchal's premium location, directly on the oceanfront with a magnificent sea-level solarium area of lush subtropical gardens with direct sea access, fountains, water cascades and swimming pools. All rooms have their own private balcony and panoramic views. 113 bedrooms.

The Vine Hotel €€ *Rua das Aranhas 27; tel: 291 009 000*; www.hotelthevine. com. A hotel with soul. Inspired by Madeira's wine-making industry, this sleek and sophisticated hotel is the brainchild of local interior designer Nini Andrade Silva. At the spa, indulge in a vinotherapy treatment that includes a red wine bath with antioxidant wine extracts. Rooms are decorated in warm muted shades and feature free-standing baths, often at the foot of the bed. A rooftop pool with bar provides panoramic views over the bay which are stunning.

FUNCHAL TOURIST ZONE

Belmond Reid's Palace €€€€ *Estrada Monumental 139, 9000 Funchal; tel: 291 717 171; tel: 800 237 1236 (US & Canada, toll-free); tel: 0845 077 2222 (UK, local call rate);* www.belmond.com. Sumptuously decorated, Madeira's legendary hotel preserves the elegance of a bygone age. The magnificent gardens overlook the sea. Spacious sun terraces, pools and tennis courts. A wide variety of packages is available, some of them surprisingly affordable at certain times of the year. Access available for travellers with disabilities. 158 rooms.

Buganvilia Studio Hotel € *Rua da Casa Branca 98; tel: 291 706 600;* www.dorisol.com/en. Superbly located, affordable family accommodation with excellent facilities. Comfortable, pristine studio rooms have a kitchenette and balcony. Outdoor and indoor swimming pool, sauna, Jacuzzi, spa, gym and tennis court. The promenade and the Lido swimming complex are within a five-minute walk. 150 rooms.

Cliff Bay Hotel €€€€ *Estrada Monumental 147, 9004-532 Funchal; tel: 888 205 7322 (US); tel: 0808 145 3788 (UK); tel: 469 610 3608 (Europe);* www.cliff-bay-resort-funchal.com. This luxurious hotel is set on a clifftop opposite the Lido supermarket. Guests are pampered with large, smartly designed rooms, most have panoramic sea and harbour views, and spacious and well equipped bathrooms. The main facilities include two pools (one of them a seawater lagoon), a spa, a tennis court, three restaurants and four bars. Disabled access. Free Wi-Fi. 200 rooms and suites.

Enotel Lido Resort €€€€ *Rua Simplício dos Passos Gouveia 29, 9004-576 Funchal; tel: 291 702 000;* www.enotel.com. An all-inclusive option, this is another of the big and bold five-star resorts to sprout along the coast in the tourist zone. It is awash with sports facilities, and all the expected comforts and services. The modern rooms, which all have balconies and sea views, are extremely plush and stunning. Access available for travellers with disabilities. 317 rooms.

Hotel Girassol € *Estrada Monumental 256, 9004 Funchal; tel: 291 701 570;* www.hotelgirassolmadeira.com. The Girassol is a modern hotel refurbished in 2020, pleasant and friendly, with a consistent package-deal clientele. The rooms are fairly basic, but each has a terrace or balcony with garden, mountain or sea views. Despite being located on the busy main Funchal highway, the hotel has secluded gardens with swimming pools. It also has three restaurants, a spa and gym. Access available for travellers with disabilities. 136 rooms.

Pensão Vila Vicência € *Rua da Casa Branca 45, 9000 Funchal; tel: 291 771 527;* www.vilavicencia.com. A delightful, family-run *pension* comprising three adjacent houses, Vila Vicência is just a five-minute walk from the Lido complex and so is found in a fantastic location. It has a lovely and tranquil little garden on-site and there is also a private swimming pool to make the most of. 29 rooms.

Pestana Palms €€ *Rua do Gorgulho 17, 9000 Funchal; tel: 291 709 200; www. pestana.com.* This aparthotel on the seafront incorporates a restaurant with amazing views of the ocean and a traditional tea house. Nicely furnished, self-catering studios, heated pool, health club, gymnasium, and free wi-fi. 76 rooms.

Pestana Village €€€ *Estrada Monumental 194, 9000 Funchal; tel: 291 701 600; www.pestana.com.* Looking rather like a well-designed village straight out of a Mexican resort, the Village Aparthotel has a faux-Moorish lobby with a mosaic floor, a beautifully landscaped swimming pool area and award-winning sub-tropical gardens with native trees. Nicely equipped studio apartment suites and a relaxing spa centre. Half-board is available. Access available for travellers with disabilities. 92 rooms.

Suite Hotel Eden Mar €€ *Rua do Gorgulho 2, 9004-537, Funchal; tel: 291 709 700; www.portobay.pt.* This well-equipped, popular and modern aparthotel is in the heart of the tourist zone. Part of the Eden Mar shopping complex, shops, bars and restaurants are on the doorstep. All studios have a kitch-enette, private balcony and sea views. Guests have access to outdoor and indoor pools set in verdant gardens, as well as squash, snooker, a health club, a spa and sauna, a sun terrace, a pleasant garden, and several restaurant and bar options. Access available for travellers with disabilities. 146 studios and rooms.

Tui Blue Madeira Gardens €€€ *Azinhaga da Casa Branca, 9004-543, Funchal; tel: 291 213 600; www.savoysignature.com.* Another fine hotel from Savoy Ho-tels & Resorts Madeira, the boutique-style, adults-only Madeira Gardens is set back from the ocean and occupies a quiet and sunny spot. It has a reading room with a library, and an extensive panoramic rooftop terrace complete with whirlpool. After dark there is nightly musical entertainment. 119 bedrooms.

VidaMar Resort Madeira €€€€ *Estrada Monumental 175–7, 9000 Funchal; tel: 291 717 700; www.vidamarresorts.com.* The hotel is formed of two towers separated by a low block with a wave-shaped roof. The decor is minimalist and stylish, and all rooms have panoramic sea views. Five restaurants and lively bars, snooker room, two indoor and four outdoor pools, a spa, and a fitness centre. Access available for travellers with disabilities. Rates are for half board. 300 rooms.

BEYOND FUNCHAL

Casa das Videiras € *Sítio Serra d'Água, 9270 Seixal; tel: 965 522 727;* http://videiras.com. Charming guesthouse in a tiny, pretty town on the north coast. This mid-nineteenth-century manor house has clean and attractively decorated rooms, and a friendly and relaxed atmosphere – a tribute to the hands-on owner. 4 rooms.

Casa do Caseiro € *Caminho do Monte 62, 9050 Funchal; tel: 291 611 031*. High above Funchal, halfway down Monte's famous toboggan run. Small, delightful, private house, attractive gardens, pool and terrace with lovely views. 7 rooms.

Casa Velha do Palheiro €€€€ *Rua da Estalagem 23, São Gonçalo, 9060 Funchal; tel: 291 790 350;* www.casa-velha.com. The only hotel in Madeira on a golf course, this handsome and stylish hotel in the hills east of Funchal occupies an 1804 country house connected to the Palheiro Gardens, part of the prestigious Palheiro Golf Club. Great city views are aplenty here, an elegant restaurant, heated pool, gym, tennis court and special golf packages. 33 rooms.

Dom Pedro Baía €€ *Estrada de São Roque, 9200 Machico; tel: 291 969 500;* www.dompedrobaiahotel.com. A modern high-rise overlooking the bay of Machico, this comfortable hotel is a good base for exploring the eastern part of the island. Popular with British and German package tours, it has a large swimming pool, a tennis court, bar and nightly entertainment. Access available for travellers with disabilities. 218 rooms.

Estalagem da Ponta do Sol €€ *Quinta da Rochinha, 9360 Ponta do Sol; tel: 291 970 200;* www.pontadosol.com. Set on the clifftop east of Ponta do Sol village, this modern boutique hotel undermines the image of Madeira as a resort for retirees. A series of white-walled cubes with plate-glass windows, the Ponta do Sol is a modernist dream. The delightful gardens and bar are located in the original mansion, while the excellent restaurant is perfectly positioned for glorious views of the sunset. 54 rooms with sea and garden views also.

Estalagem do Mar € *Sítio dos Juncos, Fajã da Areia, 9240 São Vicente; tel: 291 840 010;* www.estalagemdomar.com. Within walking distance of São Vicente, sandwiched between a sheer cliff and the roaring sea, this sprawling hotel offers exclusivity at a bargain price. Each of the simply furnished rooms faces the ocean. There is an indoor and outdoor pool, restaurant and tennis court. 91 rooms.

Estalagem Eira do Serrado € *Curral das Freiras, 9000 Funchal; tel: 291 710 060;* www.eiradoserrado.com. This four-star guesthouse with elegant rooms, all with balconies, occupies a splendid setting right on the rim of the hidden valley of Curral das Freiras. Enchanting views are guaranteed as you look down over green terraces to the isolated village in the valley far below, or up to the jagged volcanic peaks that encircle the skyline. Indoor pool, restaurant, Jacuzzi, sauna and wine cellar. 26 rooms.

Estalagem Quinta do Estreito €€€€ *Rua José Joaquim da Costa, 9325 Estreito de Câmara de Lobos; tel: 291 910 530;* www.quintadoestreitomadeira.com. A luxury *quinta*, or villa, with elegant furnishings set 400 metres (1,300ft) above sea level, overlooking the vineyards of Câmara de Lobos. A relaxing hideaway, the *quinta* has landscaped tropical gardens, comfortable, tastefully decorated rooms, and there is a restaurant, library and heated pool. 44 rooms.

Hotel Encumeada € *Feiteiras, Serra d'Água, 9350 Ribeira Brava; tel: 291 951 282.* Few places can match the setting of this unpretentious hotel. Just down the road from the Encumeada pass, it sits on a ledge overlooking the mountains and valley around Serra de Água, halfway between the north and south coasts. Ideal for walkers and hikers. 49 rooms.

Quinta do Furão €€ *Achada do Gramacho, 9230 Santana; tel: 291 570 100;* www.quintadofurao.com. Built in rustic style, this rural inn is set amid a sea of green orchards and grapevines, with views of the undulating hills around

Santana. The best hotel in the area, the 'Quinta of the Ferret' offers style and relaxation, with a cool little pool with a retractable roof, and a fine rustic restaurant. The hotel hosts a wine festival in September and is a great event to attend. 65 rooms and suites.

Residencial Amparo € *Rua da Amargura, 9200 Machico; tel: 291 968 120;* www.amparohotel.com. A simple hotel, comfortably decorated, in the centre of Machico, just two blocks from the seafront. A pleasant and personal alternative to the larger *Dom Pedro Baía* (see page 139). Attractive restaurant. 12 rooms.

Savoy Saccharum €€€€ *Rua Serra de Água 1; tel: 291 820 800;* www.savoysignature.com/saccharumhotel/en. Near the sandy Calheta beach and next to a marina, this resort sits between the mountains and the ocean. Built on the site of a sugar cane mill, the hotel has incorporated this heritage into its design. Large, elegant rooms (some with kitchenettes) have a balcony, the majority overlooking the sea. Extensive facilities include two indoor and three outdoor pools, as well as a spa, games room and a kids' club. Three restaurants and four bars, with live music, together with a terrace offering alfresco dining with ocean views. It makes for a delightful and enjoyable stay. 243 rooms and suites.

PORTO SANTO

Pestana Porto Santo €€€ *Santo Estrada Regional 163, Sítio do Campo de Baixo; tel: 291 144 000;* www.pestana.com/en/hotel/pestana-porto-santo. Eco-certified, the *Pestana Porto Santo* is a fantastic place to stay. A five-star inclusive resort, it boasts lots of attractive features. There are plenty of bars and eateries to make the most of. For relaxation, head to the spa or enjoy the pools on-site. You are also treated to direct beach access.

Torre Praia €€€ *Rua Goulart Medeiros, 9400 Porto Santo; tel: 291 980 450;* www.portosantohotels.com/torrepraia. Just outside Vila Baleira, this attractive four-star hotel has simple furnishings and overlooks Porto Santo's excellent beach and the ocean. Kidney-shaped swimming pool with separate children's section, gym, sauna and jacuzzi and three restaurants to enjoy. 66 rooms.

INDEX

THE MINI ROUGH GUIDE TO
MADEIRA

First Edition 2022

Editors: Zara Sekhavati, Philippa MacKenzie
Authors: Neil Schlecht, Maciej Zglinicki
Updater: Jackie Staddon
Picture Editor: Tom Smyth
Cartography Update: Carte
Layout: Pradeep Thapliyal
Head of DTP and Pre-Press: Katie Bennett
Head of Publishing: Kate Drynan
Photography Credits: 123RF 11, 26, 51; Bigstock
47; Dreamstime 4TR, 19, 35, 36, 55, 67, 71;
Fotolia 5M, 29, 32, 49, 53, 57, 58, 69, 75, 76, 86;
Getty Images 18, 74; iStock 5M, 30, 46, 61, 84,
90, 96, 98; Madeira Tourism 28, 40, 45, 62, 81, 88;
Madeira Tourism/Julio Marques 33; Mary Evans
Picture Library 21, 24; Orient-Express Hotels 95;
Paul Murphy/Apa Publications 4MC; Palheiro
Nature Estate 42; Phil Wood/Apa Publications
4CR, 65; Shutterstock 1, 4TL, 4TC, 4CL, 4BL, 4BR,
5T, 5C, 5B, 6T, 6B, 7T, 7B, 13, 43, 72, 76, 78, 92, 101
Cover Credits: View from Miradouro de Sao
Cristovao **Simon Dannhauer/Shutterstock**

Distribution

UK, Ireland and Europe: Apa Publications (UK)
Ltd; sales@roughguides.com
United States and Canada: Ingram Publisher
Services; ips@ingramcontent.com
Australia and New Zealand: Booktopia;
retailer@booktopia.com.au
Worldwide: Apa Publications (UK) Ltd;
sales@roughguides.com

Special Sales, Content Licensing
and CoPublishing
Rough Guides can be purchased in bulk
quantities at discounted prices. We can create
special editions, personalised jackets and
corporate imprints tailored to your needs. sales@
roughguides.com; http://roughguides.com

All Rights Reserved
© 2022 Apa Digital AG
License edition © Apa Publications Ltd UK

Printed in Spain

Contact us
Every effort has been made to provide accurate
information in this publication, but changes
are inevitable. The publisher cannot be held
responsible for any resulting loss, inconvenience
or injury sustained by any traveller as a result
of information or advice contained in the
guide. We would appreciate it if readers would
call our attention to any errors or outdated
information, or if you feel we've left something
out. Please send your comments with the subject
line "Rough Guide Mini Madeira Update" to
mail@uk.roughguides.com.